What Others Say About

Exploring the Basics of Biblical Christianity
by Neil Curran

"*Exploring the Basics of Biblical Christianity* is a biblical 'boot camp' for believers. Many how-to books have been written that help believers learn the practical disciplines of prayer and Bible study, but few focus on mastering the great truths that must under gird one's faith. Neil's work fortifies the head, the heart, and the hands. It is a systematic theology for this generation—grounded in the truth of God's Word with practical life applications."

> *Dr. Charles Dyer*
> *Provost & Senior Vice President of Education*
> *Moody Bible Institute*

"Clear. Concise. Complete. Just what the doctor ordered for newborns in Christ and those who disciple them."

> *Dr. Lewis J. Wilson*
> *Evangelism Pastor*
> *Second Baptist Church, Houston, Texas*

"Neil's book is like a Swiss Army Knife. Everything you need to understand the basics of the Bible swivels right out of this one volume. It's easy to use, it's clear, and it's to the point. And it can be used by young and old alike. This is a tool you will value and use often."

> *Steve Farrar*
> *Best selling author of* Point Man,
> *dynamic Promise Keepers conference speaker*
> *and founder of Men's Leadership Ministries.*

"I rejoice with you in this clear presentation of Bible basics."

Dr. Kenneth N. Taylor
The Living Bible and Chairman of the Board,
Tyndale House Publishers

"Every so often a truly practical tool comes along to help new believers grow in their faith. This is one of those tools, written by a man who loves to see new disciples grow. It is a simple, practical book on the basics of Christianity along with life application principles. I highly recommend this book for those who want to understand the basics of their faith."

Timothy J. Addington
Executive Director Ministry Advancement
Evangelical Free Church of America

"This is a thorough presentation of Christian doctrine from the orthodox, premillennial point of view. It is a detailed introduction to theology as it is presented in the Bible for churches desiring to have a course for their new members that introduces them to biblical truth. It will be especially helpful to new believers and those who are just starting out in the Christian life."

Dr. John F. Walvoord, Chancellor Emeritus
Dallas Theological Seminary

"Many Christians lack a solid grounding in God's Word and in sound doctrine. As a result they are not growing in the Lord and they lack spiritual power. Exploring the Basics of Biblical Christianity provides an excellent way for overcoming this problem. Studying the book will help you learn what the Bible teaches on many important topics and how you can apply these in your life. I pray that this book will be studied by many believers throughout the world."

Dr. Roy B. Zuck, Noted professor and author
Editor, Bibliotheca Sacra

"Tools like Neil Curran's Exploring the Basics of Biblical Christianity are useful for both people and preacher, the pew and the pulpit, the sheep and the shepherd."

Dr. Ramesh Richard, President, RREACH International;
Chairman, Trainers of Pastors
International Coalition (TOPIC)

"Anyone who uses it as a work book and studies through it, alone or in a small group, will come out with a fantastic understanding of Biblical and evangelical Christianity. It is the kind of thing I wish the Lord had dropped in my lap in the first years of my spiritual growth. I would have advanced much faster along with clarification of the basic doctrines."

Pastor Weldon Buwe, Birmingham, Alabama

"Exploring the Basics of Biblical Christianity is a primary tool for teaching in the Third World. It presents material in such a practical way that students can easily re-teach the same to their congregations."

Principal Phil Turley,
Moffat Bible College/AIM, Kenya, Africa

"Exploring the Basics of Biblical Christianity is a great help for new believers and those who disciple them. The doctrinal definitions and explanations and the many scriptural passages provide valuable guidance for newcomers to faith in Christ and His community of believers. The New Testament charges the Church with the solemn and joyful task of passing on the sound tradition of faith; this book is a significant resource for fulfilling that responsibility."

Dr. Stephen Spencer, Professor of Theology
Wheaton College

"This book is an unimpaired paradox: simple but systematic while profound but clear. It will provide Christians with a solid framework for future growth. It should be called Christianity for Dummies."

Franz Bibfeldt, Theologian

"Over a number of years, the church in Africa has been manned by lay persons who rely particularly on basic knowledge of the Bible. Exploring the Basics of Biblical Christianity by Neil Curran will facilitate and enlighten our pastors in leading and guiding the flock to greener pastures. This is an asset that will be utilized in seminar trainings and short term pastoral training."

Rev. Henry Ng'eno, Director, Christian Education,
Africa Gospel Church and National Director for
African Leadership and Reconciliation Ministries (ALARM),
Kenya, Africa

Exploring the Basics of Biblical Christianity

Exploring the Basics of Biblical Christianity

Put Together Basic Bible Teachings
Understand Major Themes of the Bible
Discover Practical Life Applications

For seekers,
new believers,
and growing disciples

Neil Curran

Exploring the Basics of Biblical Christianity

by
Neil Curran

ISBN 0-9648486-0-0

Printed in the United States of America

**Biblical Communications**
P.O. Box 293911
Lewisville, Texas 75029
(800) 424-7670

For more information visit our Web Site at:
www.biblicalcommunications.com

Acknowledgments

God's plan for reaching the world is through churches motivated by the Great Commission to "go and make disciples"
who will make disciples. I have been blessed as a member of
three wonderful local churches throughout my Christian
walk. I came to faith at Fellowship Bible Church in New Or-
leans where Pastors Weldon Buwe and Bil Gebhardt encouraged me to go on to seminary. I grew in my appreciation of
shepherding God's people under Pastor Neil Ashcraft at
Scofield Memorial Church in Dallas while I was attending
seminary.

I have had the privilege of serving as Pastor of Shepherding at Crossroads Bible Church in Lewisville, Texas. Senior Pastor Tim Stevenson leads a dynamic ministry of
God's people where the biblical mandate of the "priesthood
of believers" is fleshed out. The pastoral staff serves as
"equippers" and the entire body "ministers" in service to
one another, our community, and the world around us.
Tim's extraordinary vision, leadership, and teaching, along
with his gift of continually seeing and doing the right thing
from an understanding of and commitment to God's grace,
continually inspire me. The pastors, staff, and other brothers
and sisters at Crossroads have faithfully and graciously
ministered to me and my wife, children, and grandchildren.

Keith Boyer, Bill Hull, Larry Crabb, Dan Allender, and
Dick Averbeck have transparently opened their hearts and

encouraged me, providing insights into understanding people, including myself, from God's perspective while deepening my love for the Savior. Steve Farrar's talks and books helped me grow as a man. The Family Life Ministry helped me grow as a husband and father.

At a memorial service for Dr. John F. Walvoord on the campus of Dallas Theological Seminary, Dr. Charles Swindoll spoke of Dr. Walvoord as one of the giants of the Christian faith in the twentieth century. Dr. Walvoord was a great encouragement to me as this book was being developed. One of his books, *Major Bible Themes*, a one-volume condensation of Dr. Lewis Sperry Chafer's theology, was an inspiration for this book, which I hope will be useful in local churches in the twenty-first century.

The faculty at Dallas Theological Seminary has had an enormous impact on my life, from training pastors who have blessed me, to personally equipping me for ministry. There are still "giants in the land" and I have had the great blessing of learning from many of them, not only in learning how to study and understand the Bible, but also by the example of their personal devotion to God. Their names read like a role call out of Hebrews 11, "Faith's Hall of Fame." Bailey, Blue, Burns, Campbell, Cecil, Constable, Dyer, Gangel, Grant, Hannah, Hendricks, Johnson, Lawrence, Lightner, Lowery, Moyer, Pentecost, Pocock, Pyne, Robinson, Ryrie, Spencer, Swindoll, Toussaint, and Walvoord. They and others stand in a great tradition of teaching God's truth to new generations of shepherds. May God bless you all.

I owe a special thanks to two more DTS faculty members. My friend Ramesh Richard has inspired me over the years with his worldwide ministry and vision. Thank you for writing the Preface to this book.

Roy Zuck graciously made extensive editorial suggestions on the manuscript, strengthening the flow and clarifying various concepts. Thank you also for the Foreword.

This book is an attempt to build a foundation for understanding many of the basic teachings of the Bible and how they can be applied to our lives. It is also a "love letter" to all of the above for giving me so much of "the good stuff"…understanding the classic truths of God's Word. I hope this book will be used to pass the truth on to another generation of believers who will use it to impact their world for Christ.

I am grateful to Merrikay Lee and Sally Flory for their technical skills in formatting the manuscript for publication. Other friends read earlier drafts and made many helpful suggestions.

My thanks go to gifted and talented artist Matt Campbell who created the cover design and illustration.

A number of friends helped to launch the publication of the book. I am deeply grateful for their support and friendship.

Thanks to our daughter, Sheila and her husband John, our son Tom and his wife Andrea, and our grandchildren, Anna Grace, Peter, Joanna, Jonathan, Erica, and Conner, who bless me with their love for the Lord and their parents. May each of you walk with Him all of your life.

Most of all, I thank Jody, my young wife of nearly forty years. Thanks for your encouragement, partnership in ministry, friendship and love. I am blessed to be married to a woman of God.

This book is dedicated to all of you.

Neil Curran

Contents

Foreword

"I don't understand what the Bible is all about."

"The Bible is a puzzling book. People have such different ideas about the Bible's teachings."

"How can I put all the pieces of this biblical puzzle together so that it makes sense?"

Neil Curran answers these questions by providing a book that opens up the teachings of the Bible in a simple systematic way. He discusses every major doctrine of the Bible and shows how each doctrine is relevant to readers today.

Some people think doctrine is dull, dry, and irrelevant. But far from it! The doctrines (teachings) of the Bible are remarkably relevant and profoundly intriguing for they deal with the deepest questions we ever ponder. What is God like? How did the world originate? What is the purpose of life? Why are we here? How will the world end? How can we have lasting inner peace? How can we lead clean lives? Are we different from animals? Can we trust the Bible? Do demons exist? Are angels real? What is Satan trying to do? How can we have world peace? Is Jesus Christ any different from other religious leaders?

Read the contents of this book carefully. Study the doctrines thoroughly. Meditate on the verses prayerfully. And live out the implications of the doctrines enthusiastically. As you do, you will "grow in the grace and knowledge of the Lord and Savior Jesus Christ" (2 Peter 3:18).

Roy B. Zuck

Dr. Zuck is editor of *Bibliotheca Sacra*, the oldest continuously published theological journal in America. He has edited, authored, or co-authored more than 25 books, including *The Bible Knowledge Commentary*, *Adult Education in the Church*, and *Basic Bible Interpretation*. He is the former Academic Dean, Vice President for Academic Affairs, Chairman, and Senior Professor of the Bible Exposition Department at Dallas Theological Seminary.

Preface

If the solution to a busy life is simplication, and the goal of an effective ministry is multiplication, Neil Curran subscribes to both goals as the driving factors of his life and ministry.

As a fellow-servant of Almighty God and a fellow-shepherd in Christ's church, he strives to provide biblically-based convictions for Christian belief and behavior in this introductory digest of essential biblical truths.

If you would like a "Walk Through Biblical Essentials" for learning or teaching basic theological truths, this book will provide you with summaries, texts, outlines and applications.

Another major audience for the book will be found among the hundreds of thousands of pastoral leaders in developing nations ministering without formal training. Some exhibit God's calling in zeal, but do not possess biblical preparation in knowledge, and are thus open to honest whims with interpretative fancies that may disturb or even harm their congregations. An overview of foundational biblical truth will not only intensify their convictions, but increase the reach of those truths where the Church is exploding in numbers, but imploding under its own weight.

Tools like Neil Curran's "Exploring the Basics of Biblical Christianity" are useful for both people and preacher, the pew and the pulpit, the sheep and the shepherd. The author carries credibility having personally experienced what he himself needed and continues to use in ongoing pastoral ministry. I commend his desire to participate in disciple-making and to perpetuate pastoral training in this practical way.

For the Sake of His Bride, Worldwide
Ramesh Richard

Dr. Richard has two earned doctorates, a Ph.D. from the University of Delhi and a Th.D. from Dallas Theological Seminary. He has a worldwide proclamation ministry. As the founder and President of Ramesh Richard Evangelism and Church Helps (*RREACH*) International he has traveled to over 70 countries for ministry. He is also a professor at Dallas Theological Seminary and the founding Chairman of Trainers of Pastors International Coalition (TOPIC). He has authored several books including *Scripture Sculpture* and *Mending the Hole In Your Heart.* His annual New Year's Day telecast has reached tens of millions around the world with the good news of the Lord Jesus Christ.

Chapter 1

Introduction

This material is what I wished I had been able to easily put my hands on and my brain around when I was a newcomer to biblical Christianity. If you have tried to put together a jigsaw puzzle without the picture on the top of the box, you'll understand. I needed the big picture to figure out where all the pieces fit.

A friend of mine was just beginning to study the Bible for the first time. He was having trouble finding the various books of the Bible and understanding what he was reading. One day he told me, "I feel like I'm in Mexico and I only know enough Spanish to order lunch." The material in this book quickly helped him enjoy the banquet the Bible offers to all who seek it.

In a good Bible-teaching church you will get all the pieces. Eventually you will get the big picture if you do little more than come to church and listen to the sermons. If you take adult education classes, you will process more information faster. Also excellent study Bibles and reference books can help you understand the Scriptures and grow spiritually.

What this book will do is to speed the process by giving you an overview of the Bible's teachings. Your perspective of the whole determines how you view each part and what you understand. What are the important issues? Our goal is to help you discover the major themes of the Bible and begin to understand them and how they apply to your life.

Each major topic is discussed in one chapter. We will attempt to answer the question, "What?" What does the Bible have to say about this subject? We will examine the subject material and look at some of the related key Bible verses. These verses would be great ones to use as part of a Bible memorization plan for yourself. I suggest you highlight them in your own Bible for future reference. We will look at what these verses mean by discussing and explaining them, if necessary.

Then under the section "Practical Life Application" we will try to answer the question, "So what?" If this teaching is true, what does it mean to me? How should I respond? How should it affect my life? How has it affected my life before this, even if I didn't know it was true? How can I use this information in my life? What are some practical steps I can take now to implement this truth and build it into my life?

Let's walk through our Table of Contents to discover the major themes we'll be exploring in depth, chapter by chapter. The first subject is **Worldviews**.

We all have a worldview, even if we don't know we have one. Our worldview is the way we look at life and everything in it. Everything that came before us affects us. Civilizations that came before our civilization affect us. Cultures that came before the culture we live in affect us. The homes and families we grew up in affect the homes and families we live in today.

We all have a way of thinking about things we learned in life … through our parents …school… culture … television … and so forth. All these things affected us and the way we think … even if we don't think about it. We all make some presuppositions about new things that come our way based on everything that has come our way before. We make judgments and form opinions based on who we are and what we believe.

It is important to understand our own thinking process.

The Apostle Paul wrote one of our key passages in Colossians 2:8-10:

"Don't let anyone lead you astray with empty philosophy and high-sounding nonsense that comes from human thinking and from the evil powers of this world, and not from Christ. For in Christ the fullness of God lives in a human body, and you are complete through your union with Christ. He is the Lord over every ruler and authority in the universe."

The next chapter is **The Bible**.

Who wrote the Bible? And when? Is it reliable? What about the different versions and translations? Is the Bible really relevant? How can I read and study the Bible and get something out of it?

We will look at answers to all of these questions and more.

One key passage here is 2 Timothy 3:16-17:

"All Scripture is inspired by God and is useful to teach us what is true and to make us realize what is wrong in our lives. It straightens us out and teaches us to do what is right. It is God's way of preparing us in every way, fully equipped for every good thing God wants us to do."

The fourth chapter is about **God**.

If there is a God and He is good, it follows that He would want to reveal Himself to His creation. He did so, and He still does. And always will. What is He like? What about the Trinity? Where does the Bible teach about the triune God? What are our personal responsibilities before God?

The fifth chapter is about **Jesus Christ—The Person**.

Who is Jesus? Is He a man? Is He God? Is He a God/man? A teacher? A good man? Was He a crazy person who claimed to be God?

The sixth chapter is about **Jesus Christ—His Work**.

What did Jesus do on earth? What is He doing now? What does it all mean to me? How can I be sure? What is the difference between eternal security and assurance of salvation?

The seventh chapter deals with **The Holy Spirit**.

Is the Holy Spirit really God? Or a ghost? What does He want to do in my life?

In chapter eight we will be **Looking at the World from God's Point of View**.

We will take a broad view of history and how God has dealt with mankind at different times. Dispensational theology provides a clear way of seeing how God has dispensed His will and related to mankind during different ages of human history. We will look at the covenants God has made with man through the centuries, such as the Abrahamic Covenant, the Mosaic Covenant, and the New Covenant we celebrate at communion or the Lord's Supper.

The ninth chapter will focus on **The Difference between Law and Grace.** We now live under the covenant of grace, which is the New Covenant. How does this apply to our lives today? This study, often neglected or misunderstood, can free us from the bondage of legalism and false guilt.

Chapter ten is on **The Church**. What is the universal church? Who is in it? What is my role in the church? What is the difference between the local church and the universal church? We'll also explore the topic of spiritual gifts.

Chapter eleven is about **Human Beings**. What is human nature like, according to the Bible? What does God say about us? How can I understand myself and others from God's perspective? Can people really change?

The twelfth chapter is about **Christian Living**. How do you live the Christian life? How do I get from point A to point Z—from earth to heaven? How am I supposed to live? How can I be expected to live a godly life while living in an ungodly world?

Chapter thirteen is **Angels—Good and Bad**. Do you believe in angels? Do we each have a guardian angel? What about the devil? Is Satan real, or is there just an evil force in the universe? If Satan is real, what are his goals? What can he do? What should we do about him?

Chapter fourteen discusses **Things Still To Come**. What does the Bible have to say about the future? Why should I believe some of these fantastic things I have heard about the end times? How can I make sense of the Book of Revelation? Who is this Antichrist? Is there really a hell and a lake of fire? What's heaven like? Where will I spend eternity?

Chapter fifteen is **Quick Start—For New Believers**. This will help people start out on the right path after they have trusted Christ.

As you read this book, I invite you to pray over the contents. Meditate on the key verses and commit them to memory. Highlight them in your own Bible for future reference. Talk about these things with others who are studying the material at the same time, under the guidance of an experienced teacher.

Chapter 2

Worldviews

We all have a worldview, even if we have never used the term. We all have a way of thinking about the world that we have learned through life—from our homes, schools, television, movies, newspapers, books, and other people.

Even Our Sense of History Is Affected

Everything that has gone before us in world history affects the way we think, even if we don't think about it. Our sense of history is shaped by how other people describe it according to their worldviews.

Following is a quote from an international celebrity virtually everyone knows about. Yet our understanding of him and his own worldview is severely limited by what other people have written about him.

Read his own words. I will block some of the specific references to places, but see if you can guess who this person is. He could have lived thousands of years ago, hundreds of years ago, or still be alive today.

"It was the Lord who put into my mind (I could feel his hand upon me) the fact that it would be possible to 'go' from here to _____. All who heard of my project rejected it with laughter, ridiculing me. There is no question that the inspiration was from the Holy Spirit, because He comforted me with rays of marvelous inspiration from the Holy Scriptures....

"I am a most unworthy sinner, but I have cried out to the Lord for grace and mercy, and they have covered me completely. I have found the sweetest consolation since I made it my whole purpose to enjoy His marvelous presence. For the execution of the journey to the _____, I did not make use (only) of intelligence, mathematics, or maps. It is simply the fulfillment of what Isaiah had prophesied....

"No one should fear to undertake any task in the name of our Saviour, if it is just and if the intention is purely for His holy service. The working out of all things has been assigned to each person by our Lord, but it all happens according to His sovereign will, even though He gives advice. He lacks nothing that it is in the power of men to give Him. Oh, what a gracious Lord, who desires that people should perform for Him those things for which He holds Himself responsible! Day and night, moment by moment, everyone should express their most devoted gratitude to Him."

This is undoubtedly a man committed to God, a man who studied the Scriptures as a significant part of his life. Whose words are these we just read? These are the words of Christopher Columbus taken from his own journal as he sailed to the West Indies. These words were recorded by a sixteenth-century historian who was with Columbus on his third voyage.[1] Columbus also wrote his *Book of Prophecies*, which is "a compilation of the Bible's teaching about the earth, distant lands, population movements, and undiscovered tribes, as well as similarly pertinent writings of the ancient church fathers...."[2]

---

1. Bartolome de Las Casas, *The Voyages of Christopher Columbus*, trans. Cecil Jane, pp. 146-147, quoted in Peter J. Marshall Jr. and David B. Manuel Jr., *The Light and the Glory* (Old Tappan, NJ: Revell, 1977), p. 17.

The thought that Columbus searched for new lands based on references from the Bible so that he might glorify his Lord is normally not taught in our schools. Yet it is important that we know the whole truth to understand what motivated Columbus.

In our times, however, we seem to want to separate biblical things from everyday life. Unfortunately we tend to overlook the influence of the Bible in our history and society.

We All Have Presuppositions

Every one of us makes presuppositions based on life as we already know it. For much of the last century some people have tried to remove the Bible as the basis for any of our presuppositions.

James Dobson tells an anecdote that describes the impact of our presuppositions. A man was brought to him for counseling. The man was a scientist who had come to believe he had died. The man was absolutely sure he was dead. Then Dr. Dobson asked him a scientific question based on the certain knowledge that the circulatory system stops pumping blood when death occurs and the heart stops pumping. "Do dead men bleed?" asked Dobson. The man responded, "Of course not." Dobson then took out a needle and pricked the man's finger and blood dropped out. The man was amazed. He said, "How about that? Dead men do bleed!"

Our presuppositions have a powerful influence over us. We all have preconceived ideas that color our thinking. Because we believe a, b, and c, we are likely to believe d, e, and f.

---

2. Ibid., p. 360.

Our Cultural Worldview

The worldview of the United States is largely shaped by three cities today, New York, Hollywood, and Washington, D.C. The way these major metropolitan cities have influenced us over the past century has dramatically changed our society.

Think of New York as the center of news and television. We've gone from Walter Cronkite and Opie to Saturday Night Live and on to Jerry Springer and Howard Stern. If you want to, you may watch full nudity and explicit sex in your living room.

Hollywood brought us wonderful epic movies such as Cecil B. Demille's "The Ten Commandments." But today instead of leaving Egypt we are "Leaving Las Vegas" with naked "Showgirls." We've gone from the action films of Roy Rogers to "The Godfather" to the open violence and mayhem of slasher films. Many films today are dark, depraved, and depressing.

Washington, the center of our government, is no longer a model of morality. President Teddy Roosevelt used to read and quote the Bible. Even a few years ago politicians tried to hide their adulterous affairs from the public. In recent years the sexual escapades of the highest elected officials seem to be regular primetime news.

Our magazines have gone from the *Saturday Evening Post* to *Playboy* to *Hustler*. Our pop music has gone from Bing Crosby to the Kingston Trio and Elvis and on to punk rockers and gangster rap artists who glorify death and Satan.

Our society's morality has taken a downward spiral and it is now spinning downward faster and faster. This is true not only of the United States. A parallel downward spiral is happening in most of the world's metropolitan centers. We must return to a biblical worldview.

The following chart, inspired by material from Probe Ministries, outlines the major worldviews of our day and what they teach about key issues.

	Comparison of Worldviews				
ıue	Secular/ Humanist/ Relativist	Existential/ Post-modernism	New Age/ Pantheism	Biblical Christianity	Key Scripture Verses
ıd	There is no god.	Probably no god. Irrelevant.	All is God. A force.	There is one God.	Deut. 6:4
ıd's Nature	Superstition.	If God exists, He is in-competent or evil.	Impersonal / Amoral.	Personal/ Moral.	Gen. 17:1
e Universe	Matter / Energy.	Absurd.	Everything is god.	Created by God.	Gen. 1:1
ᵤth/ ıowledge	Reason / Science. Man is the measure.	Irrational / Elusive.	Truth is within us.	Truth is revealed by God (naturally and specifically.)	Rom. 1:19-20 John 1:14-18
ıman Beings	Evolved animals.	Accidents.	Spiritual beings, gods.	Created in God's im-age but fallen.	Gen. 1:27 Gen. 3:16-19
ᵢics	Relative / Situational. If it feels good, do it.	Pointless.	Relative.	Absolutes.	Isaiah 55:8-9 Proverbs
ıman ᵢoblem	Ignorance.	Meaninglessness.	Bad karma. Unenlightened.	Sin. Selfishness. Rebellion against God.	Isaiah 59:2 Rom. 3:23 Rom. 6:23
ılution to ᵢoblem	Education.	None.	Raised consciousness. Enlightenment.	The Savior. Faith in and obedience to the Lord Jesus Christ.	John 3:16 Rom. 5:8 I Cor. 15:1-6
ᵢstory	Linear but chaotic.	Accidental.	Cyclical.	Linear but providential.	2 Cor. 5:18-21 Isaiah 45:5-6 Isaiah 49:6 I Cor. 15:28
ᵢath	End of existence.	Inevitable.	Reincarnation.	Eternal reward or eternal suffering.	Rev. 20:10-15
ᵢligion	Some good moral influence.	Superstition.	All roads lead to the same place.	Jesus Christ is the only one path to God.	John 14:6 Acts 4:12
ᵢsus Christ	Moral teacher.	Irrelevant myth.	One of many guides, teachers, avatars, gurus to God.	The unique, fully God, fully man Lord and Savior.	John 1:1 John 1:14 Rev. 19:11-16
ᵢntemporary ᵢpressions	Values clarification. Abortion rights. Dominates media, government, and education.	Post-war and anti-war movements. Youth culture. Alien-ation. Drugs.	Channeling. The occult. Horoscopes. Animal rights equal or sur-pass human rights. Hyper-environmentalism.	Evangelical, Bible-believing, born-again Christians.	

"Don't let anyone lead you astray with empty philosophy and high-sounding nonsense that come from human thinking and from the evil powers of this world, and not from Christ. For in Christ the fullness of God lives in a human body, and you are complete through your union with Christ. He is the Lord over every ruler and authority in the universe."   (Colossians 2:8-10)

Biblical Christianity Worldview - Key Scripture Verses

God

"Hear, O Israel! The LORD is our God, the LORD alone" (Deuteronomy 6:4).

God's Nature

"When Abram was ninety-nine years old, the LORD appeared to him and said, 'I am God Almighty; serve me faithfully and live a blameless life,'" (Genesis 17:1).

The Universe

"In the beginning God created the heavens and the earth" (Genesis 1:1).

Truth/Knowledge

"For the truth about God is known to them instinctively. God has put this knowledge in their hearts. [20]From the time the world was created, people have seen the earth and sky and all that God made. They can clearly see his invisible qualities—his eternal power and divine nature. So they have no excuse whatsoever for not knowing God" (Romans 1:19-20).

"So the Word became human and lived here on earth among us. He was full of unfailing love and faithfulness. And we have seen his glory, the glory of the only Son of the Father.

[15]"John pointed him out to the people. He shouted to the crowds, 'This is the one I was talking about when I said, "someone is coming who is far greater than I am, for he existed long before I did,' [16]We have all benefited from the rich blessings he brought to us—one gracious blessing after another. [17]For the law was given through Moses; God's unfailing love and faithfulness came through Jesus Christ. [18]No one has ever seen God. But his only Son, who is himself God, is near to the Father's heart; he has told us about him" (John 1:14-18).

Human Beings

"So God created people in his own image; God patterned them after himself; male and female he created them" (Genesis 1:27).

"Then he said to the woman, 'You will bear children with intense pain and suffering. And though your desire will be for your husband, he will be your master.' [17]And to Adam he said, 'Because you listened to your wife and ate the fruit I told you not to eat, I have placed a curse on the ground. All your life you will struggle to scratch a living from it. [18]It will grow thorns and thistles for you, though you will eat of its grains. [19]All your life you will sweat to produce food, until your dying day. Then you will return to the ground from which you came. For you were made from dust, and to the dust you will return" (Genesis 3:16-19).

Ethics

"'My thoughts are completely different from yours,' says the LORD. 'And my ways are far beyond anything you could imagine. For just as the heavens are higher than the earth, so are my ways higher than your ways and my thoughts higher than your thoughts'" (Isaiah 55:8-9).

Human Problem

"But there is a problem—your sins have cut you off from God. Because of your sin, he has turned away and will not listen anymore" (Isaiah 59:2).

"For all have sinned; all fall short of God's glorious standard" (Romans 3:23).

"For the wages of sin is death" (Romans 6:23).

Solution to Problem

"But the free gift of God is eternal life through Christ Jesus our Lord" (Romans 6:23).

"But God showed his great love for us by sending Christ to die for us while we were still sinners" (Romans 5:8).

"Jesus replied, 'I assure you, unless you are born again, you can never see the Kingdom of God'" (John 3:3).

"For God so loved the world that he gave his only Son, so that everyone who believes in him will not perish but have eternal life" (John 3:16).

"Now let me remind you, dear brothers and sisters, of the Good News I preached to you before. You welcomed it then and still do now, for your faith is built on this wonderful message. ²And it is this Good News that saves you if you firmly believe it— unless, of course, you believed something that was never true in the first place.

³"I passed on to you what was most important and what had also been passed on to me—that Christ died for our sins, just as the Scriptures said. ⁴He was buried, and he was raised from the dead on the third day, as the Scriptures said. ⁵He was seen by Peter and then by the twelve apostles. ⁶After that, he was seen by more than five hundred of his followers at one time, most of whom are still alive, though some have died by now" (1 Corinthians 15:1-6).

History

"All this newness of life is from God, who brought us back to himself through what Christ did. And God has given us the task of reconciling people to him. [19]For God was in Christ, reconciling the world to himself, no longer counting people's sins against them. This is the wonderful message he has given us to tell others. [20]We are Christ's ambassadors, and God is using us to speak to you. We urge you, as though Christ himself were here pleading with you, 'Be reconciled to God!' [21]For God made Christ, who never sinned, to be the offering for our sin, so that we could be made right with God through Christ" (2 Corinthians 5:18-21).

"I am the LORD; there is no other God. I have prepared you, even though you do not know me, [6]so all the world from east to west will know there is no other God. I am the LORD, and there is no other" (Isaiah 45:5-6).

"He says, 'You will do more than restore the people of Israel to me. I will make you a light to the Gentiles, and you will bring my salvation to the ends of the earth'" (Isaiah 49:6).

"Then, when he has conquered all things, the Son will present himself to God, so that God, who gave his Son authority over all things, will be utterly supreme over everything everywhere" (1 Corinthians 15:28).

Death

"Then the Devil, who betrayed them, was thrown into the lake of fire that burns with sulfur, joining the beast and the false prophet. There they will be tormented day and night forever and ever. [11]And I saw a great white throne, and I saw the one who was sitting on it. The earth and sky fled from his presence, but they found no place to hide. [12]I saw the dead, both great and small, standing before God's throne. And the books were opened, including the Book of Life. And the dead were judged according to the things written in the books, according to what they had done. [13]The sea gave up the dead in it, and death and the grave gave up the dead in them. They were all judged according to their deeds. [14]And death and the grave were thrown into the lake of fire. This is the second death—the lake of fire. [15]And anyone whose name was not found recorded in the Book of Life was thrown into the lake of fire" (Revelation 20:10–15).

Religion

"Jesus told him, 'I am the way, the truth, and the life. No one can come to the Father except through me'" (John 14:6).

"There is salvation in no one else! There is no other name in all of heaven for people to call on to save them" (Acts 4:12).

Jesus Christ

"In the beginning the Word already existed. He was with God, and he was God. [2]He was in the beginning with God. [3]He created everything there is. Nothing exists that he didn't make. [4]Life itself was in him, and this life gives light to everyone" (John 1:1-4).

"So the Word became human and lived here on earth among us. He was full of unfailing love and faithfulness. And we have seen his glory, the glory of the only Son of the Father" (John 1:14).

"Then I saw heaven opened, and a white horse was standing there. And the one sitting on the horse was named Faithful and True. For he judges fairly and then goes to war. [12]His eyes were bright like flames of fire, and on his head were many crowns. A name was written on him, and only he knew what it meant. [13]He was clothed with a robe dipped in blood, and his title was the Word of God. [14]The armies of heaven, dressed in pure white linen, followed him on white horses. [15]From his mouth came a sharp sword, and with it he struck down the nations. He ruled them with an iron rod, and he trod the winepress of the fierce wrath of almighty

God. [16]On his robe and thigh was written this title: King of kings and Lord of lords" (Revelation 19:11-16).

Practical Life Application

Do you have a biblical worldview? Do you stop and evaluate things from God's point of view? How can you line up your life with God's will?

The more you read and study God's Word, the Bible, the more you will get to know Him and what He wants. As you step faithfully in obedience to what you learn, God will reveal more and more to you from His Word and enable you to do more. If you do not obey His Word, you should not expect more light.

It is important for Christians to gather together, not only on Sunday mornings in worship services, but also in small groups where relationships can be built and lives opened up to help one another. We can learn from other more mature Christians.

This book is a good place to capture the big picture of God's point of view on the world. It will help you understand many of the basic themes of the Bible and help you see how to live more wisely and in accord with God's will in your everyday life and help you make plans for the future.

Chapter 3

The Bible

In the last chapter we examined the concept of worldviews. As we saw, our presuppositions give us the worldview by which we evaluate new information and decide how to act and live.

Suppose an angel sent a fax to several major newspapers with the message, "God says the world will end tomorrow."

The *New York Times* would probably read like this: "The world will end tomorrow, says a reliable source." A box on the page might read, "Analysis on page 11." Differing worldviews might be expressed in these headlines:

The *Wall Street Journal* might read: "World ends tomorrow; market plunges!"

U.S.A. Today: "We're gone!"

And the *Washington Post*: "World ends tomorrow; Congress approves term limits and school prayer."[1]

What about our own worldview? As Christians we need to explore how we should run our worldview through one

1. Cal and Rose Samra, *Holy Humor* (New York: MasterMedia and the Fellowship of Merry Christians, 1996), p. 19.

more filter, one more grid of information. We need to examine the world from God's point of view.

What Is God's Worldview?

In the Old Testament, the prophet Isaiah wrote a message from God: "'My thoughts are completely different from yours,' says the LORD. 'And my ways are far beyond anything you could imagine. [9]For just as the heavens are higher than the earth, so are my ways higher than your ways and my thoughts higher than your thoughts'" (Isaiah 55:8-9).

Can we understand God's viewpoint?

We can because He is a God of revelation. He reveals Himself to us so we can understand Him. It makes sense that the Creator would want His creation to know Him. God has revealed Himself to people in two basic ways: natural revelation and special revelation.

Natural Revelation

Natural revelation comes from the universe we live in. We can understand there is a Creator by looking at the world around us. It is obvious there is someone bigger than us.

Psalm 19:1-4 says, "The heavens tell of the glory of God. The skies display his marvelous craftsmanship.[2]Day after day they continue to speak; night after night they make him known.[3]They speak without a sound or a word; their voice is silent in the skies; [4]yet their message has gone out to all the earth and their words to all the world. The sun lives in the heavens where God placed it."

And the apostle Paul wrote in the Book of Romans, "For the truth about God is known to them instinctively. God has put this knowledge in their hearts. [20]From the time the world was created, people have seen the earth and sky and all that God made. They can clearly see his invisible qualities—his eternal power and divine nature. So they have no excuse whatsoever for not knowing God. [21]Yes, they knew God, but they wouldn't worship him as God or even give him thanks. And they began to think up foolish ideas of what God was like. The result was that their minds became dark and confused. [22]Claiming to be wise, they became utter fools instead. [23]And instead of worshipping the glorious, ever-living God, they worshipped idols made to look like mere people, or birds and animals and snakes" (Romans 1:19-23).

Special Revelation

So all men are without excuse for not seeking after God. God reached down to mankind even more directly through what we call special revelation. He did this in three ways: the spoken word to the prophets and apostles; the written Word, or Bible; and the Living Word, Jesus Christ.

Jonah was an Old Testament prophet. His book begins, "The LORD gave this message to Jonah son of Amittai" (Jonah 1:1). The New International Version translates this, "The word of the Lord came to Jonah." The King James translates passages of God's messages to His prophets as "Thus saith the Lord."

In the Old Testament there are dozens of references to God speaking to prophets in audible words, dreams, and visions. We have their accounts in writing.

In Exodus 17:14 we read, "Then the LORD instructed Moses, 'Write this down as a permanent record, and announce it to Joshua'" In Exodus 34:27 the Bible says, "And the LORD said to Moses, 'Write down all these instructions, for they represent the terms of my covenant with you and with Israel.'"

This chapter focuses on the written Word of God, what we call the Scriptures or the Bible.

Basic Information about the Bible

If you landed on some remote jungle island where the natives had never been exposed to Western civilization or Christianity, what would you tell them about the Bible?

What would you tell your neighbors today?

The Bible was written over a time span of more than 1,500 years, from about 1,400 B.C. to about A.D. 96. Some forty different human authors wrote the various books or letters which make up the Bible. The Greek word *biblia* is plural for "books." There are two major divisions. The Old Testament has thirty-nine books and the New Testament has twenty-seven books. There are sixty-six books in all.

The chart on the next page lists all the books by category for easy reference.

The Old Testament

Most of the Old Testament was written in Hebrew. Some portions of Ezra and Daniel are in Aramaic, a language similar to Hebrew. The Old Testament deals primarily with God's covenant with Israel. Moses is recognized as the author of the first five books, which detail God's creation of the universe, the earth, and mankind. They then tell about God's selection of the Jewish people through one man, Abram or Abraham, through the time of Moses, the exodus from Egypt, issuing of the Ten Commandments and the whole Mosaic Law, until the "chosen people" were about to enter the Promised Land, Israel. The rest of the Old Testament recounts the history of the people and God's interaction with them until about four hundred years before the birth of Jesus Christ. It includes law, history, government, poetry, wisdom literature, and prophecy. One of the major themes in the Old Testament is a promise of a coming King who would save Israel. This Savior is called the Messiah, the anointed One of God.

The Bible at a Glance (66 Books)[2]

OLD TESTAMENT (39 Books)			"The New is in the Old concealed. The Old is in the New revealed."	NEW TESTMENT (27 Books)		
History 17 Books	Poetry 5 Books	Prophecy 17 Books	*The Old Testament*	History 5 Books	Teaching 21 Books	Prophecy 1 Book
Law Genesis Exodus Leviticus Numbers Deuteronomy	Job Psalms Proverbs Ecclesiastes Song of Solomon	**Major Prophets** Isaiah Jeremiah Lamentations Ezekiel Daniel	*looks forward to Christ's sacrifice on the cross.*	**Gospels** Matthew Mark Luke John	**Paul's Letters** Romans 1 Corinthians 2 Corinthians Galatians Ephesians	Revelation
History and Government Joshua Judges Ruth 1 Samuel 2 Samuel 1 Kings 2 Kings 1 Chronicles 2 Chronicles Ezra Nehmiah Esther		**Minor Prophets** Hosea Joel Amos Obadiah Jonah Micah Nahum Habakkuk Zephaniah Haggai Zechariah Malachi	*The New Testament is based on the work Christ finished on the cross.* *About 400 years between the Testaments.*	Acts	Phillipians Colossians 1 Thessalonians 2 Thessalonians 1 Timothy 2 Timothy Titus Philemon **General Letters** Hebrews James 1 Peter 2 Peter 1 John 2 John 3 John Jude	

God used about 40 different men over a period of 1,500 years (from about 1,400 B.C. to A.D. 96.) in writing the Bible.

The Apocrypha

The Roman Catholic Bible differs in that it adds seven books and parts of two more books to the Old Testament. These additions, called the Apocrypha, were written by Jewish authors within a few hundred years before the life of Christ. They were not formally added to the official Roman Catholic list until A.D. 1546 by the Council of Trent. The

---

2.   Friendship Bible Coffee Bible Studies, Stonecroft Ministries.

Jewish Bible (what Christians call the Old Testament) never acknowledged these additions as an official part of God's Word. Neither did early church fathers such as Jerome, who translated the Bible from its original languages into Latin in the fifth century. Protestant translations never included the Apocrypha. It is important to note that Jesus and the apostles, while often quoting from the Old Testament, never once quoted from the Apocrypha as a source of authority.

The New Testament

The New Testament was written in Greek, the language of the Mediterranean world after the conquests of Alexander the Great. These books contain the writings of the apostles and their close associates. The first four books are known as the Gospels, four accounts of the life and teachings of Jesus. The Book of Acts describes the historical events from Christ's ascension to heaven through the spread of Christianity beyond Israel to other parts of the Roman Empire. Most of the rest of the New Testament is in the form of letters, called epistles, from apostles like Peter and Paul to the churches in different cities around the Mediterranean. The Bible concludes with the apostle John's "Revelation" (or the "Apocalypse"), which is about his eyewitness account of Jesus, short messages to several churches, and a grand vision and prophecy of the future when Christ will return to reign in majesty and the unbelieving world will be judged.

The Bible Is Unique

The Bible is an amazing and unique book. Even though it was written over fifteen centuries by about forty different authors, the Bible has remarkable internal consistency. The later authors quote earlier writers. In Genesis, the very first book of the Bible, God promised to send a Deliverer. The thread of redemption to come with that Deliverer or Savior runs throughout the Old Testament. The fulfillment of that promise comes to fruition with the birth, crucifixion, and resurrection of Jesus, the promised Messiah or Christ. The

Old and New Testaments form one complete book. The first is incomplete and neither can be fully understood without knowledge of the other.

History confirms the Bible's uniqueness. It has been the best-selling book for hundreds of years. Over six billion copies have been printed. Portions of it have been translated into more than 2,800 languages. It has survived persecution and outright banning. From the beginning the Bible has had a unique impact on people. God has used His Word to draw people to Himself and to change lives. It is read over and over again. It becomes a lifelong companion and changes many individuals' worldviews, ethics, relationships, and lives.

Is the Bible We Have Accurate and Reliable?

God has supernaturally protected the Bible over the centuries. We can be sure the copies we have in our language today are faithful expressions of the message God gave to the world through His prophets and apostles.

Dead Sea Scrolls

When the Dead Sea Scrolls were discovered after World War II in clay jars hidden in a cave almost two thousand years earlier, some thought the findings would show that the Bible is false. To the contrary, these two-thousand-year-old manuscripts of the Old Testament and other writings demonstrate the remarkable accuracy of the Old Testament. Religious scribes carefully copied the sacred books of Scripture so that what we have today is virtually identical to the original manuscripts of the Bible. There is no significant difference that would change any meaning or doctrine found in the Old and New Testaments.

Archeological Discoveries

A few centuries ago many people thought the Bible was a collection of myths because many of the nations and tribes described in the historical accounts were not mentioned elsewhere in historical records. The advances in archaeology in the past two hundred years have supported the biblical record. People thought the story of Jonah was a "fish story" because there was no record of the city of Nineveh, where Jonah reportedly went to preach his message of repentance. In the late nineteenth century archaeologists discovered the buried site of Nineveh, capital of the Assyrian Empire. It was a city of many thousands of people, with walls scores of feet high and wide enough for three chariots to run abreast. Until 1906 all other records, other than the Bible, of the Hittites were nonexistent, when an archaeological dig proved the accuracy of the biblical account. No archaeological discovery has ever disproved anything in the Bible.

Reliable Ancient Manuscripts

The Bible is the most reliable book of antiquity. One of the ways of deciding reliability is to know how close in time to the original writings are the copies we have and how many different copies we have. No scholar disputes the work of Aristotle, yet we have only five early copies of his work and the oldest is a copy made 1,400 years after he died. We have seven old copies of Plato's writings, but the oldest is dated 1,200 years after Plato. No one doubts that Julius Caesar wrote "Gallic Wars," and yet we have only ten copies, and the best is dated 1,000 years after Caesar.

Would you be satisfied to have five, seven, or ten ancient copies of the New Testament to authenticate its reliability? How about a hundred? Or a thousand? We have over 24,000 ancient Greek manuscripts of parts of the New Testament! Some date to within a hundred years of Christ or within thirty years of the apostle John's writings.

The early church fathers of the second and third centuries quoted from all but eleven verses in the New Testament.

Fulfilled Prophecy Is
a Proof of the Reliability of the Bible

Hundreds of prophecies in the Bible have come true. Others are still waiting for fulfillment. Many of the prophecies have to do with the coming of the Messiah, Jesus Christ. We will look at many of these when we study Jesus Christ—the Person in chapter 5.

Some of these prophecies include the prediction of His virgin birth seven hundred years before it happened. (See Isaiah 7:14 fulfilled in Matthew 1:18-23.) Also the exact birthplace of Christ was predicted seven hundred years earlier. (See Micah 5:2 fulfilled in Luke 2:4-7.) The description of execution by crucifixion in Psalm 22 is hundreds of years older than the invention of this form of torture and execution. The description of Christ's suffering was predicted by Isaiah seven hundred years earlier. (Isaiah 53:4-6.)

Eyewitness Accounts

The Bible contains many accounts of miracles. Jesus Christ did extraordinary things, including raising people from the dead. His healings were known throughout Israel, which is why crowds followed Him everywhere. Eyewitnesses reported His miracles. The early New Testament letters were widely circulated and read aloud to the churches. There is no historical evidence of anyone trying to dispute the miracles and discredit Jesus. They dared not do so because many eyewitnesses were still alive.

The Church and the Bible

Some people think the Bible was written centuries after the establishment of the church. As we have discussed, the Bible was written by Hebrew prophets and Christ's disciples. Apostolic authority was one of the authenticating requirements for a letter or book to be accepted into the official list of New Testament books. Other letters were also circulated and some were accepted by a church here and there, but not universally. How did the Bible we have today come to include sixty-six books?

The thirty-nine books of the Old Testament were accepted by the Jewish scholars who translated the writings from Hebrew to Greek just before the time of Christ. Jesus and the apostles quoted from these books frequently, as recorded in the New Testament. In the fourth century the complete official canon was agreed on and the twenty-seven books of the New Testament were recognized as such. Athanasius, bishop of Alexandria, Egypt, sent a letter in A.D. 365 naming the twenty-seven books. The church council held at Carthage under Augustine, bishop of Hippo, agreed with this list in A.D. 397. The official Bible we have wasn't created in the fourth century; it was simply recognized as being the completed and authoritative word of God.

Isaiah wrote, "The grass withers, and the flowers fade, but the word of our God stands forever" (Isaiah 40:8). And Jesus said, "Heaven and earth will disappear, but my words will remain forever" (Matthew 24:35).

The Inspiration of Scripture

The Apostle Paul, in writing to his disciple Timothy, said in 2 Timothy 3:14-17:

"But you must remain faithful to the things you have been taught. You know they are true, for you know you can trust those who taught you. [15]You have been taught the holy Scriptures from childhood, and they have given you the wisdom to receive the salvation that comes by trusting in Christ Jesus. [16]All Scripture is inspired by God and is useful to teach us what is true and to make us realize what is wrong in our lives. It straightens us out and teaches us to do what is right. [17]It is God's way of preparing us in every way, fully equipped for every good thing God wants us to do."

"All Scripture is inspired by God." The New International Version translates this, "All Scripture is God-breathed." Because of our own modern ideas about inspiration, I like to use the phrase "God-breathed" when talking about the Bible. Some writers of novels and poetry were inspired. But only the Scriptures are God-breathed.

Jesus called the Scriptures "God's message" (John 10:35). He accepted it as the Word of God.

These references have to do with the Old Testament. What about the New Testament?

In Ephesians 3:3-5, Paul said, "As I briefly mentioned earlier in this letter, God himself revealed his secret plan to me. [4]As you read what I have written, you will understand what I know about this plan regarding Christ. [5]God did not reveal it to previous generations, but now he has revealed it by the Holy Spirit to his holy apostles and prophets."

The apostle Peter, writing in 2 Peter 3:16, acknowledged Paul's writings as Scripture. In 2 Peter 1:20-21, Peter wrote, "Above all, you must understand that no prophecy in Scripture ever came from the prophets themselves[21]or because they wanted to prophesy. It was the Holy Spirit who moved the prophets to speak from God."

The concept of the Holy Spirit moving the prophets comes from a Greek sailing term. It is like the wind and water moving or carrying along a sailboat. A sailboat can't move under its own power. In the same way, men were moved by the Holy Spirit to write the very words of Scripture. The Bible is a direct revelation from God. It is His word to us.

Inspiration of Scripture Defined

An excellent definition of the inspiration of Scripture has been provided by Charles Ryrie, author of *The Ryrie Study Bible*. He writes, "Inspiration is the act by which God superintended the human authors of the Bible so that they composed and recorded without error His message to mankind in the words of their original writings."[3]

---

3.   Charles C. Ryrie, *Basic Theology* (Wheaton, IL: Victor Books), 1986, p. 71.

Verbal, Plenary Inerrant Inspiration

Conservative, evangelical Christians believe in verbal, plenary, inerrant inspiration of Scripture. Let's examine this doctrine.

Verbal: the very words themselves

Plenary: all the words, every one of them, the entire Bible, not just portions of it

Inerrant: without error

Inspiration: God-breathed

Scripture: God's message to us, the Bible, Old and New Testaments

Christians should take the Bible seriously. God does.

Translations of the Bible

The Bible was given to us by God so that His people could read it, listen to it being taught, study it, memorize it, and have it impact their lives. It was written long ago in languages the average person of the day could understand but few people in the world speak today. Of necessity, then, the Bible must be translated into the common languages of people around the globe. Languages themselves change with time. The English-speaking world no longer uses the same English used by people in Shakespeare's time. It has changed over the centuries. If the Bible is to be read by people today, it should read as easily as the daily newspaper.

Groups of scholars, proficient in the original languages, knowledgeable about ancient customs and schooled in theology, have often gathered to update and modernize translations of the Bible in many languages. Most of these translations are sound and reliable.

The following information on Ephesians 2:12, developed by Dr. Andy Black, may help in understanding the translation process.

Translation Analysis of Ephesians 2:12[4]

(minus the first word "that" or "because"

Original Greek[5]

etE toù Èkairoù eÈkelnoù xoùÈris Èxristu, apellatrioÈmenol tes paliÈtelas tu israÈel kai ÈksEnol toùn diaTeÈkoùn tes epaNgEÈlias, ElÈpida me ÈExontEs kal ÈaTeol En tol Èkosmoù.

Word-for-Word (Simple)

Were the time that without Christ alienated the citizenship the Israel and strangers the covenants the promise hope not having and god-less in the world.

Word-for-Word (Not So Simple)

You were in the time that without Christ alienated of the citizenship of the Israel and strangers of the covenants of the promise hope not having and godless in the world.

New American Standard Bible (NASB)

You were at that time separate from Christ, excluded from the commonwealth of Israel, and strangers to the covenants of promise, having no hope and without God in the world.

New International Version (NIV)

Remember that at the time you were separate from Christ, excluded from citizenship in Israel and foreigners to the covenants of the promise, without hope and without God in the world.

New Living Translation (NLT)

In those days you were living apart from Christ. You were excluded from God's people, Israel, and you did not know the promises God had made to them. You lived in this world without God and without hope.

This material illustrates the need for considering the way languages work in order to get the translation to communicate well and naturally.

---

4. Developed by Dr. H. Andrew Black of SIL International and used with permission.
5. The Koine Greek is used here in the International Phonetic Alphabet.

Illumination

Inspiration deals with the method of how God recorded the Scriptures. Illumination has to do with the meaning of the Scriptures. The Holy Spirit illumines (gives light) to believers as to what the Bible means.

Non-Christians talk about difficulty in understanding the Bible. Since the Bible is God's Word to His people, for an unbeliever to try and understand the Bible is almost the same as if they tried to read someone else's mail. A personal letter to someone from a loved one would have many personal references. The person for whom it was intended might understand it perfectly, but someone else would miss understanding many parts of it.

Paul wrote about this in 1 Corinthians 2:10-15. "But we know these things because God has revealed them to us by his Spirit, and his Spirit searches out everything and shows us even God's deep secrets. [11]No one can know what anyone else is really thinking except that person alone, and no one can know God's thoughts except God's own Spirit. [12]And God has actually given us his Spirit (not the world's spirit) so we can know the wonderful things God has freely given us. [13]When we tell you this, we do not use words of human wisdom. We speak words given to us by the Spirit, using the Spirit's words to explain spiritual truths. [14]But people who aren't Christians can't understand these truths from God's Spirit. It all sounds foolish to them because only those who have the Spirit can understand what the Spirit means. [15]We who have the Spirit understand these things, but others can't understand us at all."

And Paul explained why unbelievers can't fully understand the Bible. "If the Good News we preach is veiled from anyone, it is a sign that they are perishing. [4]Satan, the god of this evil world, has blinded the minds of those who don't believe, so they are unable to see the glorious light of the Good News that is shining upon them. They don't understand the message we preach about the glory of Christ, who is the exact likeness of God" (2 Corinthians 4:3-4).

The divine author of the Bible, God the Holy Spirit, indwells every Christian and guides us into understanding what He wrote. If you are a Christian, "Your body is the temple of the Holy Spirit, who lives in you" (1 Cor. 6:19). The apostle John wrote that the Holy Spirit "will guide you into all truth" (John 16:13).

Interpretation

The art of interpretation is called "hermeneutics." If you follow these basic rules of interpretation, you should be able to understand what the Bible means by what it says. (1) Pray that the Holy Spirit will guide you to understand the Scriptures. (2) Accept the normal and customary sense of the language (the literal, grammatical, historical method of interpretation.) (3) Take what you read in context. (4) Remember that no part of Scripture contradicts another and that all the parts fit perfectly into the whole. (5) Remember the chapter divisions were not in the original writings and many thoughts bridge over the chapter divisions we have in our Bibles today, which were added for reference purposes and our convenience.

Reference Helps

Many excellent tools are available to help you understand the Bible. Many are now included in CD libraries for your computer. Purchase a good study Bible with reference notes and maps. *The Open Bible* and *The Ryrie Study Bible* are two excellent ones. A complete concordance listing every word in the Bible is a handy tool. You'll also want to have a good Bible dictionary. Thousands of commentaries have been written to help explain the Bible and individual books of the Bible. The *Bible Knowledge Commentary*, written by the faculty of Dallas Theological Seminary, is an excellent two-volume set, one book covering the Old Testament and the other the New Testament. Talk with one of your pastors or elders for other suggestions.

Practical Life Application

Since the Bible is God's Word to you, what should you do about it? Obviously you should be reading the Bible. It is best to do it systematically and repetitively. Don't start in the beginning with the Book of Genesis and go from there. Instead start with the Gospel of John or the Gospel of Luke. Set aside periods of time in your week when you can sit and read undisturbed for a while. Some do it early in the morning and others at night before going to bed. Find a place where you're comfortable. Make it your special place for "a quiet time" with God. Read one of the Gospels several times. Then pick a short book in the New Testament like Philippians. Read Philippians every day for a month. After a few days, jot down notes or questions you have on a notepad you keep with your Bible. Look for answers in your study Bible or in a commentary. Ask another Christian who's been studying the Scriptures for a longer time. If your pastor is preaching through a book of the Bible, you might want to read ahead in that book so you'll understand it better. It is probably a good idea to read the whole New Testament before you tackle the Old Testament. Start your Old Testament reading in the Psalms or the Book of Proverbs. Or read some of these passages as you read through the New Testament.

Plan your time of study. Read. Reflect on what you have read. What did you just learn? Pray for an opportunity to put what you learned into practice. Reflect on what you have done according to God's Word. Your evaluation will bring maturity and wisdom.

Your reading will give you knowledge. Reflection will help you think it through and give you understanding of that knowledge. Practice what you've learned. Put it to use in your life. Then evaluate the results. This will help you grow in maturity and build your life on God's wisdom.

Bible Study Techniques

When you study the Bible, ask yourselves eight questions. The first four come under the heading "Observation." This applies if you are studying the whole of the Bible as a unit, one book of the Bible, a section or one chapter, or even one verse. Try it.

Under "Observation" ask four questions. Who? Where? When? What?

(1) Who wrote this? To whom was it written? Who are the people in this passage?

(2) Where is the location of the setting? Where was this book written? Is there movement from one place to another?

(3) When was the book written? When did the events in the passage occur? Was it past, present, or future from the time of the writing? From today?

(4) What is going on in the passage?

Remember, you are just observing the passage now. Don't try to figure out what it means yet.

The next step is "Interpretation." Under this heading seek to answer the questions, Why? And what does it mean? Some things are obvious. You may find it helpful to consult a commentary on this passage. What you are looking for here is the meaning the author intended for his original audience. What did it mean to them? Why did he write it?

Many books of the Bible have key verses that tell us why they were written. In the Gospel of John we have to go to the next-to-last chapter to find it. "Jesus' disciples saw him do many other miraculous signs besides the ones recorded in this book. But these are written so that you may believe that Jesus is the Messiah, the Son of God, and that by believing in him you will have life" (John 20:30-31).

Now we are ready for "Application." Here the questions to ask are, "So what? What does this mean to me? Now what should I do? Make a list of things you can do as a result of this teaching.

Take a passage like Acts 1:8 and try these techniques. "But when the Holy Spirit has come upon you, you will receive power and will tell people about me everywhere—in Jerusalem, throughout Judea, in Samaria, and to the ends of the earth."

Paul wrote to Timothy that he should apply the teachings to his life "so that everyone will see your progress" (1 Timothy 4:15). Don't worry about being perfect. Progress, not perfection, is the model for the Christian life.

Chapter 4

God

Three elderly women were sitting in the park one day, bragging about their sons, each one trying to outdo the other. The first woman proudly said, "My son is a priest. When he walks into a room everyone calls him 'Father.'"

Not to be outdone, the second woman said, "My son is a bishop. When he walks into a room everyone says, 'Your Excellency.'"

The third woman smiled and said, "My son is six foot nine and weighs three hundred fifty pounds. When he walks into a room, everyone says, 'Oh, my God!'"

We all have some ideas of who God is and what He's like. Take a few minutes to think about God. Write out a definition as best you can right now. In your own words write an answer to the question What is God like? Stop reading here and pause for a minute. Write your definition.

We'll get back to your definition of God after looking at some other ideas.

The Symptoms and Solution to the World's Problems

The following article was written by a man who was deeply disturbed by what he saw going on in society around him.

He wrote, "I wish my eyes were an unlimited fountain of tears so I could cry day and night for all the people murdered in my country. I wish I had a place far out in the country so I could get away from the people and all of their corruption and pollution and moral filth. The country is filled with adulterers and unfaithful men. They shoot lies out of their mouths like bullets from a machine gun. Lies, not truth, prevail in the land today. They go from one evil deed to another."

This sounds like it could have been in this morning's newspaper.

Twenty-five hundred years ago the prophet Jeremiah, known as the weeping prophet because he was so saddened by the sinfulness of his nation Judah, wrote those words, or something very close to them, as I paraphrased them from Jeremiah 9:1-3. Those symptoms have plagued mankind for centuries.

In verse 3 Jeremiah went beyond describing the symptoms and named the root problem. "They care nothing for me, says the LORD." The New International Version translates this passage as follows: "they do not know Me, declares the LORD."

Truly knowing God is the answer to life's problems.

But is that what man thinks or does?   No, the world is looking to three things to solve all its problems: education, power, and wealth.

Jeremiah continued, "This is what the LORD says: Let not the wise man gloat in his wisdom, or the mighty man in his might, or the rich man in his riches. [24]Let them boast in this alone: that they truly know me and understand that I am the LORD who is just and righteous, whose love is unfailing, and that I delight in these things. I, the LORD, have spoken!" (Jer. 9:23-24).

God says the answer to the terrible problems we face in our society won't be solved by educating sinful people, or by how much power or how much money we have. The real solution to the world's problems comes from truly knowing God and obeying his instructions.

Do you remember at some point in your own life realizing you were very much like your parents, even if you weren't consciously trying to be like them? It's amazing, isn't it? We are around our parents so much as children we can't help but pick up their ways.

Pastor, author, and seminary chancellor Charles Swindoll writes, "That's the way it is with God our Father. The more I get to know my God, the more I become like Him. I discover He's holy; I want to be holy. I discover He's good; I want to be better. I want to be like my Father. And in order to be like Him, I need to know what He's like."[1]

How do we *know* God?

Psalm 19:1 says, "The heavens tell of the glory of God. The skies display his marvelous craftsmanship."

We can know something *about* God by looking at His work—the world around us—all creation. That's natural revelation.

And as we saw earlier, in 2 Timothy 3:16: "All Scripture is inspired by God [God-breathed] and is useful to teach us what is true."

The very words of the Bible are God-breathed. They are God's word to us. The Bible is His special revelation in which He has revealed Himself to us so we can know Him. The best place to learn about God and get to know Him is in the Bible.

---

1. Charles R. Swindoll, *Growing Deep in the Christian Life* (Grand Rapids: Zondervan Publishing House, 1997), p. 94.

The Essence of God

God possesses certain inherent attributes or essential qualities of God.

1. God is an immaterial and infinite spirit.

   "God is spirit"(John 4:24).

   "ghosts—or spirits—don't have bodies" (Luke 24:39).

2. God is invisible.

   "No one has ever seen God" (John 1:18).

   "No one has ever seen Him, nor ever will" (1 Timothy 6:16).

3. God is alive.

   Joshua 3:10; Psalm 84:2; Revelation 7:2

   Having life means having feeling, power, activity (Ps. 115:3)

4. God is a person.

   He has:

   ▸ Self-consciousness (Exod. 3:14; 1 Cor. 2:10)
   ▸ Self-determination (Job 23:13; Rom. 9:11)
   ▸ Intellect (Gen. 18:19; Acts 15:18)
   ▸ Sensitivity (John 3:16)
   ▸ Will (Gen. 3:15)

5. God is self-existent.
   "I Am the One Who Always Is"…"I am who I am" (Exod. 3:14, NIV).

6. God is immense.

   Both immanent (near) and transcendent (above all) (Acts 17:24-28).

7. God is eternal. "The Eternal God" (Gen. 21:33).

The Attributes of God

1. God is omnipresent, that is, present everywhere at once (Ps. 139:8).

2. God is omniscient, that is, all knowing, of everything past, present, and future (Ps. 147:4-5).

3. God is omnipotent, that is, all powerful (Gen. 17:1, "Almighty God.") God can do anything which is in harmony with His perfect nature. (He even has the power of self-limitation.)

4. God is immutable, that is, unchanging (James 1:17).

5. God is holy (Lev. 11:44-45; 1 Pet. 1:16; John 17:11).

6. God is righteous and just (Gen. 18:25).

7. God is true (Deut. 32:4; John 17:3).

8. God is love (1 John 4:8).
    (Goodness, kindness, mercy and grace flow from His love.)

The Sovereignty of God is Absolute

The story of Babylonian King Nebuchadnezzar, the most powerful man in the world at his time, demonstrates the absolute authority and sovereignty of God. Here's how the prophet Daniel recorded it.

"But all these things did happen to King Nebuchadnezzar. ²⁹Twelve months later, he was taking a walk on the flat roof of the royal palace in Babylon. ³⁰As he looked out across the city, he said, 'Just look at this great city of Babylon! I, by my own mighty power, have built this beautiful city as my royal residence and as an expression of my royal splendor.'

³¹"While he was still speaking these words, a voice called down from heaven, 'O King Nebuchadnezzar, this message is for you! You are no longer ruler of this kingdom. ³²You will be driven from human society. You will live in the fields

with the wild animals, and you will eat grass like a cow. Seven periods of time will pass while you live this way, until you learn that the Most High rules over the kingdoms of the world and gives them to anyone he chooses.'

[33]"That very same hour the prophecy was fulfilled, and Nebuchadnezzar was driven from human society. He ate grass like a cow, and he was drenched with the dew of heaven. He lived this way until his hair was as long as eagles' feathers and his nails were like birds' claws.

[34]"After this time had passed, I, Nebuchadnezzar, looked up to heaven. My sanity returned, and I praised and worshipped the Most High and honored the one who lives forever. His rule is everlasting, and his kingdom is eternal.[35]All the people of the earth are nothing compared to him. He has the power to do as he pleases among the angels of heaven and with those who live on earth. No one can stop him or challenge him, saying, 'What do you mean by doing these things?'

[36]"When my sanity returned to me, so did my honor and glory and kingdom. My advisers and officers sought me out, and I was reestablished as head of my kingdom, with even greater honor than before.

[37]"Now I, Nebuchadnezzar, praise and glorify and honor the King of heaven. All his acts are just and true, and he is able to humble those who are proud" (Daniel 4:28-37).

The biblical account of Nebuchadnezzar's fall and restoration is usually not taught in secular history books. To acknowledge God's authority over this great king would mean that God has authority over us today. Some people refuse to yield to God.

"The attributes of God make clear that God is supreme over all. He yields to no other power, authority, or glory, and is not subject to any absolute greater than

Himself. He represents perfection to an infinite degree in every aspect of His being. He can never be surprised, defeated, or uncertain. However, without sacrificing His authority or jeopardizing the final realization of His perfect will, it has pleased God to give to men a measure of freedom of choice, and for the exercise of this choice God holds man responsible."

Lewis Sperry Chafer ²

The Names of God

1. Old Testament

Jehovah or *Yahweh*—Gen. 2:4; Exod. 3:13-14 ("I Am the One Who Always Is"…"I am who I am," NIV)
elohim—Gen. 1:1 ("strong one" a plural form)
adonai—("master" or "lord")

Some combinations of these names include these:

Jehovah-jireh, "The Lord will provide" (Gen. 22:13-14)

Jehovah-rapha, "The Lord who heals" (Exod. 15:26)

Jehovah-shalom, "The Lord our peace" (Judg. 6:24)

2. New Testament

The Father

The Son

The Holy Spirit

---

2. Lewis Sperry Chafer and John F. Walvoord, *Major Bible Themes* (Grand Rapids: Zondervan Publishing House, 1974), p. 42.

The Trinity

Several passages in the New Testament speak of the triune Godhead, the Trinity, the fact that God exists as three persons in one.

1. Matthew 3:16-17—The baptism of Jesus

"After his baptism, as Jesus came up out of the water, the heavens were opened and he saw the Spirit of God descending like a dove and settling on him. [17]And a voice from heaven said, 'This is my beloved Son, and I am fully pleased with him.'"

2. Matthew 28:18-19—The great commission

"Jesus came and told his disciples, 'I have been given complete authority in heaven and on earth. [19]Therefore, go and make disciples of all the nations, baptizing them in the name of the Father and the Son and the Holy Spirit. [20]Teach these new disciples to obey all the commands I have given you. And be sure of this: I am with you always, even to the end of the age.'"

3. Galatians 4:6-7—Sonship comes only through Christ

Writing to those who trusted Christ, Paul said, "And because you Gentiles have become his children, God has sent the Spirit of his Son into your hearts, and now you can call God your dear Father (Abba, Father.) [7]Now you are no longer a slave but God's own child. And since you are his child, everything he has belongs to you."

Some people mistakenly teach that God is everyone's Father and therefore everyone will go to heaven. The Bible clearly teaches that only those who believe in Christ for salvation are the sons of God in a spiritual sense, and that is the only way to heaven.

"But to all who believed him and accepted him (the Lord Jesus Christ), he gave the right to become children of God. [13]They are reborn! This is not a physical birth resulting from human passion or plan—this rebirth comes from God" (John 1:11-12).

Through the centuries, Christian theologians have sought to explain and define the Trinity. The doctrine of the Trinity was agreed on in A.D. 381 at the church council held in Constantinople.

The Creed of Constantinople (A.D. 381)

"We believe in one God, the Father All Governing, creator of heaven and earth, of all things visible and invisible;

"And in one Lord Jesus Christ, the only-begotten Son of God, begotten from the Father before all time, Light from Light, true God from true God, begotten not created, of the same essence (reality) as the Father, through Whom all things came into being, Who for us men and because of our salvation came down from heaven, and was incarnate by the Holy Spirit and the Virgin Mary and became human. He was crucified for us under Pontius Pilate, and suffered and was buried, and rose on the third day, according to the Scriptures, and ascended to heaven, and sits on the right hand of the Father, and will come again with glory to judge the living and dead. His Kingdom shall have no end.

"And in the Holy Spirit, the Lord and life-giver, Who proceeds from the Father [and the Son[3]], Who is worshipped and glorified together with the Father and Son, Who spoke through the prophets; and in one, holy, catholic [universal], and apostolic Church. We confess one baptism for the remission of sins. We look forward to the resurrection of the dead and the life of the world to come. Amen."

---

3. This phrase was added by the Synod of Toledo in 589 as agreed by the church fathers in Western or Latin church but not in the Eastern church. This was part of the disagreement that caused the split between the churches in the East and the West.

The "baptism" here refers to the baptism of the Holy Spirit which occurs the moment a person trusts Christ. This is not referring to any ritual of water baptism. We'll deal with this subject in more depth later.

Procession of Father, Son, and Holy Spirit

In the New Testament the Father is presented as the First Person of the Trinity. The Father sends and commissions the Son, who is presented therefore as the second person of the Trinity. The Father and the Son send and commission the Holy Spirit, the third person of the Trinity. This is called the doctrine of procession. If you look at this process in reverse, the Holy Spirit points to the Son and the Son points to the Father.

Roles of Each Person of the Trinity

The New Testament defines and reveals the full doctrine of the Trinity.

1. The Father is presented as electing, loving, and bestowing. He appears as the planner.

2. The Son is presented as suffering, redeeming, and upholding the universe. He appears to be the doer, the active Word of God.

3. The Holy Spirit is presented as regenerating, indwelling, baptizing, energizing, and sanctifying. He appears to be God's agent in the world today, the power source living within each believer.

The Challenge of the Trinity

Biblical Christianity teaches the Trinity has unity, diversity, and equality: three persons in one God. The challenge comes from trying to maintain each from their opposite as illustrated by the triangle below: **unity**—one God (not tritheism or three gods); **diversity**—three persons (not just one God with three roles); and **equality**—each person of the

Godhead is fully God (not that some parts of the Trinity are subordinated or are less God than other parts).

Not Subordination
(Some of the Trinity is less than God)

Unity   Diversity

Orthodoxy
(Biblical Christianity)

Equality

Not Modalism   Not Tritheism
(One God...3 roles)   (3 Gods) [4]

Take a look at your original definition of God. How do you think you would change it now?

Practical Life Application

Now what? Read Matthew 11:28-30. "Then Jesus said, 'Come to me, all of you who are weary and carry heavy burdens, and I will give you rest. [29]Take my yoke upon you. Let me teach you, because I am humble and gentle, and you will find rest for your souls. [30]For my yoke fits perfectly, and the burden I give you is light.'"

Are you trusting God for everything in your life? What might you be holding back?

Read Psalm 31:1-24. Write down your personal reflections.

How can we get to know God better? What specific steps will you take to accomplish this?

Make a date with your spouse or a close friend. Talk about if and how you are really growing in your knowledge of God. Are you walking more closely with Jesus Christ now than last year or five years ago?

---

4. John Hannah, illustration from class notes, "History of Doctrine," Dallas Theological Seminary. Used with permission.

How will you change your priorities and your schedule in the coming weeks to learn more about God and to walk closer with Christ?

As you read through some of the passages mentioned in this lesson, ask God to deepen your understanding and vision of who He is.

What would you dream God could accomplish through your life? We read in 2 Chronicles 16:9: "The eyes of the LORD search the whole earth in order to strengthen those whose hearts are fully committed to him..."

Chapter 5

Jesus Christ–The Person

Who is the person we call Jesus Christ? In this chapter we will look at Jesus Christ—not what He did, but who He is. The New Testament presents seven aspects of the person of Jesus Christ.

1. The Preincarnate Christ

The apostle John opens his Gospel by saying, "In the beginning the Word already existed. He was with God, and he was God" (John 1:1). John added, "So the Word became human and lived here on earth among us" (John 1:14).

In John 8:53-58, he described an encounter between the Jewish religious leaders and Jesus. "'Are you greater than our father Abraham, who died? Are you greater than the prophets, who died? Who do you think you are?'

[54]"Jesus answered, 'If I am merely boasting about myself, it doesn't count. But it is my Father who says these glorious things about me. You say, 'He is our God,' [55]but you do not even know him. I know him. If I said otherwise, I would be as great a liar as you! But it is true—I know him and obey him. [56]Your ancestor Abraham rejoiced as he looked forward to my coming. He saw it and was glad.'

[57]"The people said, 'You aren't even fifty years old. How can you say you have seen Abraham?'"

[58]"Jesus answered, 'The truth is, I existed before Abraham was even born!' [59]At that point they picked up stones to kill him. But Jesus hid himself from them and left the Temple."

These verses speak of the preincarnate Christ. He existed in heaven before He was born on planet earth. The New American Standard Bible translates part of this passage this way: "Before Abraham was born, I am." Jesus used the same words God spoke to Moses in Exodus 3:14 when Moses, hiding his face from the burning bush, asked God what His name was. God said to Moses, "I AM THE ONE WHO ALWAYS IS."

Jesus was claiming to be the historic God of Israel, Yahweh, God Himself. The Jewish leaders knew exactly what Jesus meant. They thought it was blasphemy and they wanted to kill Him right there by stoning Him to death, the penalty for blasphemy. Only God could claim to be God. And if Jesus wasn't God, He must have been insane or a liar. He didn't leave us any other options. But He did leave us with evidence recorded by eyewitnesses in the New Testament that He is indeed God.

2. The Incarnate Christ

On the previous page we noted part of John 1:14. Here is the complete verse. "So the Word became human and lived here on earth among us. He was full of unfailing love and faithfulness. And we have seen his glory, the glory of the only Son of the Father." Other translations say the Word became "flesh." John was referring to the human birth of Jesus to the virgin Mary. Jesus lived among them for more than thirty years. John was an eyewitness to the life of Jesus and saw Him "full of unfailing love and faithfulness." John was also there with Peter and James on the Mount of Transfiguration and saw Jesus glorified. He heard the voice of God the

Father say from a cloud, "This is my Son, my Chosen One. Listen to him" (Luke 9:28-35). John again saw the glorified Christ, as he recorded in Revelation 1:13-18.

"He was wearing a long robe with a gold sash across his chest. [14]His head and his hair were white like wool, as white as snow. And his eyes were bright like flames of fire. [15]His feet were as bright as bronze refined in a furnace, and his voice thundered like mighty ocean waves. [16]He held seven stars in his right hand, and a sharp two-edged sword came from his mouth. And his face was as bright as the sun in all its brilliance.

[17]"When I saw him, I fell at his feet as dead. But he laid his right hand on me and said, 'Don't be afraid! I am the First and the Last. [18]I am the living one who died. Look, I am alive forever and ever! And I hold the keys of death and the grave.'"

Some early church traditions indicate John and Jesus were first cousins. John's mother is named in the Bible as Salome. She too was a disciple of Christ. Salome was at the crucifixion (Matt. 27:56 and Mark 15:40), and she brought burial spices to the tomb (Mark 16:1). Salome's sister, according to other early sources, was Mary. Even if this tradition of their kinship is not documented in the Bible, there is no question that Jesus and John were very close and loved each other. The apostle John was perhaps the closest man to Jesus during His earthly life. He knew Jesus in the flesh. When he saw Jesus in his glory, John "fell at his feet" (Rev. 1:17).

The theological term *incarnate* comes from a Latin word for "flesh." It means to have flesh. Chili is a meal made with beans. When you add meat to chili you get chili con carne...chili with meat. Jesus is God in human flesh so that we can see and understand Him and relate to Him as He relates to us.

Another theological term worthy of examination is the "hypostatic union."

The "hypostatic union"

=

Christ's undiminished deity

and

His perfect (sinless) humanity
united in one Person forever,

Jesus the Christ
("Christ" being Greek for the Hebrew
"Messiah" or "the Anointed One")

I remember hearing Major Ian Thomas, author and founder of the Torchbearer schools around the globe, teach that Jesus is what man was designed to be—a glorious reflection of what God is like so that all creation would see it and marvel. In Christ the whole fullness of deity dwells. He is the physical, visible, and audible picture of God. As we look at the work of Christ in the next chapter, we will see that Christ came to restore humanity to its real purpose. Christ did not come simply to get people into heaven but also to get heaven's glory into people. This is accomplished by the Spirit of Christ who comes to live in us at the moment of salvation. In Romans 8:29-30, Paul taught that we will then one day be glorified and conformed to the image of Christ.

Three other aspects of the person of Jesus Christ need to be explained.

A. The Eternal Sonship of Christ

In John 3:16 we read, "For God so loved the world that he gave his only Son, so that everyone who believes in him will not perish but have eternal life." The word "son" is from the Greek word *huios*, which refers to an heir destined to receive an inheritance. This verse does not use the word *teknos*, of Jesus, for that word refers to a believer, who is a child of God.

B. Firstborn Son of God

Romans 8:29 says, "For God knew his people in advance, and he chose them to become like his Son, so that his Son would be the firstborn, with many brothers and sisters." The Greek word for "firstborn" is *prototokos*. It has nothing to do with natural birth; it is used to signify rank, position, or pre-eminence.

C. Only Begotten Son of God

Many older translations use the word "begotten" as in "For God so loved the world that He gave His only begotten Son, that who ever believes in Him should not perish, but have eternal life" (John 3:16, NASB).

The New International Version uses the phrase "one and only Son." The New Living Translation simply uses "the only Son." The Greek word translated "only" or "only begotten" is *monogenes* (mono, "one," plus genes, "kind") and refers to His uniqueness. Jesus Christ was one of a kind—the one and only same kind as God—the only one. There is no concept of generation or birth in the word.

Other Key Verses about the Incarnation

"When Jesus came to the region of Caesarea Philippi, he asked his disciples, 'Who do people say that the Son of Man is?'

[14]"'Well,' they replied, 'some say John the Baptist, some say Elijah, and others say Jeremiah or one of the other prophets.'

[15]"Then he asked them, 'Who do you say I am?'

[16]"Simon Peter answered, 'You are the Messiah, the Son of the living God.'

[17]"Jesus replied, 'You are blessed, Simon son of John, because my Father in heaven has revealed this to you. You did not learn this from any human being'" (Matthew 16:13-17).

"Christ is the visible image of the invisible God. He existed before God made anything at all and is supreme over all creation. [16]Christ is the one through whom God created everything in heaven and earth. He made the things we can see and the things we can't see—kings, kingdoms, rulers, and authorities. Everything has been created through him and for him. [17]He existed before everything else began, and he holds all creation together.

[18]Christ is the head of the church, which is his body. He is the first of all who will rise from the dead, so he is first in everything. [19]For God in all his fullness was pleased to live in Christ, [20]and by him God reconciled everything to himself. He made peace with everything in heaven and on earth by means of his blood on the cross. [21]This includes you who were once so far away from God. You were his enemies, separated from him by your evil thoughts and actions, [22]yet now he has brought you back as his friends. He has done this through his death on the cross in his own human body. As a result, he has brought you into the very presence of God, and you are holy and blameless as you stand before him without a single fault" (Colossians 1:15-22).

Jesus Christ is God. He is the Creator of heaven and earth, in fact the Creator of everything. He is the atomic "glue" that holds everything together. One day you and I will stand before Him, and He will welcome us into His heavenly presence.

3. Christ in His Death

Jesus Christ not only lived a human life here on earth; He also died a horrible death by crucifixion. His blood stopped circulating. He stopped breathing. He was pronounced dead by his professional executioners. He was taken away and buried. Read John 19.

4. The Resurrected Christ

The last chapter of each of the Gospels reports Jesus' resurrection. In John's Gospel, the last two chapters (20 and 21) describe events after the resurrection. The first chapter of the Book of Acts also speaks of Jesus' days after the resurrection. For about forty days after His resurrection He appeared, at least ten times, to several groups of people. He appeared to large numbers of people, including up to five hundred at one time. He was real, not invisible or immaterial. Yet He walked through walls and disappeared at will. He also ate food and talked with people. The resurrected Jesus Christ was not just an apparition. He appeared in Jerusalem and some sixty miles away on the shore of the Sea of Galilee. He even told the resurrection-doubting apostle Thomas to touch His wounds and thus prove to himself the truth of His resurrection. Thomas looked closely and fell to his knees saying, "My Lord and my God!" (John 20:28).

5. Christ in Heaven

Jesus, meeting with His disciples on the Mount of Olives outside of Jerusalem, commissioned them to tell people about Him all over the world. It was not long after He said this that He was taken up into the sky while they were watching, and he disappeared into a cloud. [10]As they were straining their eyes to see him, two white-robed men suddenly stood there among them. [11]They said, 'Men of Galilee, why are you standing here staring at the sky? Jesus has been taken away from you into heaven. And someday, just as you saw him go, he will return!'" (Acts 1:9-11).

"Here is the main point: Our High Priest [Jesus Christ] sat down in the place of highest honor in heaven, at God's right hand" (Hebrews 8:1).

Jesus ascended into heaven to sit at the right hand of God the Father's throne. He is there today in His resurrected body.

6. The Return of Christ

We will discuss this subject in more detail later, but it is important to note here that the Bible talks about Christ's return for His church (believing people alive on earth) in an event called the "Rapture."

"And now, brothers and sisters, I want you to know what will happen to the Christians who have died so you will not be full of sorrow like people who have no hope. [14]For since we believe that Jesus died and was raised to life again, we also believe that when Jesus comes, God will bring back with Jesus all the Christians who have died.

[15]"I can tell you this directly from the Lord: We who are still living when the Lord returns will not rise to meet him ahead of those who are in their graves. [16]For the Lord himself will come down from heaven with a commanding shout, with the call of the archangel, and with the trumpet call of God. First, all the Christians who have died will rise from their graves. [17]Then, together with them, we who are still alive and remain on the earth will be caught up in the clouds to meet the Lord in the air and remain with him forever. [18]So comfort and encourage each other with these words." (1 Thessalonians 4:13-17).

For a period of seven years, while there is celebration in heaven (the wedding feast of Christ and His bride the church, along with an awards ceremony called "The Bema") there will be great trouble and tribulation on earth. At the end of this seven-year period Christ will return to earth with His church. Read Revelation 19 for more details. Again, we will discuss this subject in depth later on in chapter 14.

7. Christ Ruling as King of Kings

In 2 Samuel 7, God promised King David his throne would endure forever. One day a descendent of David will rule the entire earth from David's throne in Jerusalem. That has not happened yet but God's promises are true. Jesus, the promised

Messiah of Israel, is a direct descendent of David, as verified in the genealogies at his birth (see Matthew 1 and Luke 3.)

In Revelation 20:11 through 22:5 we see the fulfillment of this promise. Jesus Christ will rule from David's throne for a thousand years (the millennial kingdom) and then for eternity in the New Jerusalem and the new earth.

Three Proofs of the Deity of Christ

1. Fulfilled Prophecy

Over 320 Old Testament prophecies were literally fulfilled in Jesus Christ. The statistical probabilities of anyone but God doing this are virtually impossible.

The chart on the next page lists some of the Old Testament prophecies that were fulfilled by Christ in His first advent.

2. Miracles Performed

There is a story about a scientist who challenged God. The scientist said mankind no longer needed God because science had learned to create and clone living things. He even challenged God to a contest. God went first. He scooped up a handful of dirt, breathed on it and created a man. The scientist bent down to pick up some dirt, but God said to him, "Get your own dirt!"

Jesus performed at least thirty-five miracles, as documented in the New Testament Gospels. These included changing the molecular structure of elements (changing water into wine), successfully commanding the weather to change, storms and winds to stop and seas to calm, healing the blind and paralyzed, and raising the dead. These were supernatural events. People all over Israel witnessed them. No one doubted that miracles occurred. In fact, even the religious leaders acknowledged that Jesus performed miracles, but they claimed He did so through the power of Satan.

Prophetic Statements about Christ
from the Old Testament Confirmed in the New[1]

Messiah to enter Jerusalem on a donkey	Zechariah 9:9	Matthew 21:1-10
Messiah to be pierced	Zechariah 12:10; Psalm 22:16	John 19:34, 37
Gentiles to seek the Messiah of Israel	Isaiah 11:10	Romans 11:25
Messiah to be seed of the woman	Genesis 3:15	Galatians 4:4
Messiah to be the seed of Abraham	Genesis 12:3; 18:18	Luke 3:34; Matthew 1:2; Acts 3:25; Galatians 3:16
Messiah to be of the tribe of Judah	Genesis 49:10	Luke 3:33; Matthew 1:2
Messiah to be of the seed of Jacob	Numbers 24:17,19	Matthew 1:2; Luke 3:34
Messiah to be of the seed of David	Psalm 132:11; Isaiah 11:10; Jeremiah 23:5; 33:15	Matthew 1:6; Luke 1:32-33; Acts 2:30; Romans 1:3
Messiah to be a prophet like Moses	Deuteronomy 18:15,19	Matthew 21:11; John 1:45; 6:14; Acts 3:22-23
Messiah to be the Son of God	Psalm 2:7 (Proverbs 30:4)	Luke 1:32; Matthew 3:17
Messiah to be raised from the dead	Psalm 16:10	Acts 13:35-37
Messiah to be crucified	Psalm 22; 69:21	Matthew 27:34-50; John 19:28-30
Messiah to ascend to heaven	Psalm 68:18	Luke 24:51; Acts 1:9
Messiah to receive homage and tribute from great kings	Psalm 72:10-11	Matthew 2:1-11
Messiah to be a priest like Melchizedek	Psalm 110:4	Hebrews 5:5-6
Messiah to be at the right hand of God	Psalm 110:1	Matthew 26:64; Hebrews 1:3
Messiah to be the stone the builders rejected to become the head cornerstone	Psalm 118:22-23; Isaiah 8:14-15; 28:16	Matthew 21:42-43; Acts 4:11; Romans 9:32-33; Ephesians 2:20; I Peter 2:6-8
Messiah to be born of a virgin	Isaiah 7:14	Matthew 1:18-25; Luke 1:26-35
Galilee to be the first area of Messiah's ministry	Isaiah 9:1-8	Matthew 4:12-16
Messiah to be meek and mild	Isaiah 42:2-3; 53:7	Matthew 12:18-20; 26:62-63
Messiah to minister to the Gentiles	Isaiah 42:1; 49:1-8	Matthew 12:21
Messiah to be smitten	Isaiah 50:6	Matthew 26:67; 27:26; 30
The Gospel according to Isaiah (The suffering Messiah brings salvation)	Isaiah 52:13 – 53:12	The four gospels
The New and Everlasting Covenant	Isaiah 55:3-4; Jeremiah 31:31-33	Matthew 26:28; Mark 14:24; Luke 22:20; Hebrews 8:6-13
Twofold mission of the Messiah	Isaiah 61:1-11	Luke 4:16-21
Messiah to perform miracles	Isaiah 35:5-6	John 11:47; Matthew 11:3-6
Messiah to be called "the Lord"	Jeremiah 23:5-6	Acts 2:36
The time of Messiah's coming prophesied	Daniel 9:24-26	Galatians 4:4; Ephesians 1:10
Messiah to be born in Bethlehem	Micah 5:2	Matthew 2:1; Luke 2:4-6

---

1.   Mark Bailey, The Gospels, course notes, Dallas Theological Seminary, 1993. Used with permission.

Miracles of Christ[2]

Miracle	Place	Matthew	Mark	Luke	John
1 Turning water into wine	Cana				2:1-11
2 Healing the Nobleman's son	Capernaum				4:46-54
3 Deliverance of demoniac in synagogue	Capernaum		1:21-28	4:33-37	
4 Healing Peter's mother-in-law	Capernaum	8:14-15	1:29-31	4:38-39	
5 First miraculous draught of fish	Sea of Galilee			5:1-11	
6 Cleansing of the leper	Galilee	8:2-4	1:40-45	5:12-15	
7 Healing of the paralytic	Capernaum	9:1-8	2:1-12	5:17-26	
8 Healing infirmed man at Bethesda	Jerusalem				5:1-15
9 Healing of a man's withered hand	Galilee	12:9-13	3:1-5	6:6-ll	
10 Healing of the centurion's servant	Capernaum	8:5-13		7:1-10	
11 Raising a widow's son	Nain			7:11-17	
12 Casting out a blind and dumb spirit	Galilee	2:22-32		11:14-26	
13 Stilling the storm	Sea of Galilee	8:23-27	4:35-41	8:22-25	
14 Deliverance from demon possession	Gadara	8:28-34	5:1-20	8:26-39	
15 Healing of a woman with an issue of blood	Capernaum	9:20-22	5:25-34	8:43-48	
16 Raising Jairus' daughter	Capernaum	9:18-26	5:22-43	8:41-56	
17 Healing two blind men	Capernaum	9:27-31			
18 Casting out a dumb spirit	Capernaum	9:32-34			
19 Feeding the five thousand	Bethsaida	14:13-21	6:32-44	9:10-17	6:1-14
20 Jesus walking on the water	Sea of Galilee	14:22-33	6:45-52		6:15-21
21 Casting a demon out of a Gentile's daughter	Phoenicia	15:21-28	7:24-30		
22 Healing of a deaf and dumb man	Decapolis		7:31-37		
23 Feeding the four thousand	Decapolis	15:29-38	8:1-9		
24 Healing of a blind man at Bethsaida	Bethsaida		8:22-26		
25 Casting a demon out of a lunatic boy	Mt. Hermon	17:14-21	9:14-29	9:37-42	
26 Providing the coin in the fish's mouth	Capernaum	7:24-27			
27 Healing of a man born blind	Jerusalem				9:1-41
28 Healing of a woman with an 18-year malady	Perea (?)			13:10-17	
29 Healing a man with dropsy	Perea			14:1-6	
30 Raising Lazarus from the dead	Bethany				11:1-46
31 Cleansing of ten lepers	Samaria			17:11-19	
32 Healing of blind Bartimaeus	Jericho	20:29-33	10:46-52	18:35-43	
33 Cursing of the fig tree	Jerusalem	21:18,19	11:12-26		
34 Healing of Malchus's ear	Jerusalem			22:49-51	
35 Second miraculous draught of fish	Sea of Galilee				21:1-12

---

2.   Dr. Mark Bailey, *Miracles of Christ,* course notes, Dallas Theological Seminary, 1991. Used with permission.

3. His Bodily Resurrection

As we note earlier, the resurrected Christ was seen by as many people in at least ten postresurrection appearances. When the books of the New Testament were written and being widely circulated, many of these eyewitnesses were still alive. There is no evidence of anyone disproving the historical resurrection of Jesus Christ from death.

Other Key Verses on the Deity of Christ

"But to His Son he says, 'Your throne, O God, endures forever and ever'" (Hebrews 1:8).

"That is why I said that you will die in your sins; for unless you believe that I am who I say I am, you will die in your sins" (John 8:24).

"Jesus answered, 'The truth is, I existed before Abraham was even born'" (John 8:58).

Christ Never Sinned

The sinless quality of Jesus Christ is called the doctrine of impeccability. This word is taken from the Latin *peccatum*, which means "sin." The Savior could not and did not sin.

"This High Priest of ours understands our weaknesses, for he faced all of the same temptations we do, **yet he did not sin**. ¹⁶So let us come boldly to the throne of our gracious God. There we will receive his mercy, and we will find grace to help us when we need it" (Hebrews 4:15-16).

"And you know that Jesus came to take away our sins, for **there is no sin in him**" (1 John 3:5).

Why did Jesus Christ Have to be Both Fully Human and Fully God?

Christ had to be fully human, yet, without sin, in order to be our substitute for sin. The goats and bulls of the Old Testament sacrificial system never took away anyone's sins.

They simply covered them up for a period of time. Only a perfect human substitute could serve as the full payment for our sins. Also Christ had to be fully God in order to forgive us. Only God can forgive sins.

Practical Life Application

Who do you say He is? There are only three alternatives:

A. Jesus was wrong but did not know it. Therefore he was a lunatic.

B. Jesus was wrong and knew it. Therefore he was a liar.

C. Jesus was right. Therefore He is God.

What have you done with Jesus Christ? What do you need to do?

Have you believed on Him—trusted Him—for your eternal salvation?

Is He the Lord of your life?

What part of your life have you not given over to Him?

When will you submit to Him in this area?

If you have trusted Jesus Christ as your Savior, then He is in the process of sanctifying you. That is, He is in the process of making you like Him, holy, special, set apart for God. Some people think they have to work hard and labor to be sanctified. Actually we are sanctified the same way we are justified. Not one of us earned our justification or right standing with God. We simply accepted His free gift of salvation. In the same way, we simply need to yield to God, acknowledging our need for Him to sanctify us. As we yield our will to His will, we become sanctified. Eventually we will be glorified. We will look at all of this in greater depth later.

Others have illustrated the process by using our homes. We may have consciously invited Jesus Christ into our homes but we want to keep Him in the living room, which we think we have cleaned up for Him. But He is Lord. He keeps wanting to enter the other rooms and closets we had hoped to keep to ourselves for now.

What do you have hidden away in that back closet that He wants to clean out? Can you really invite Jesus to sit and watch your cable television channels with you? Even your favorite network shows? How good and healthy is the selection of food in your kitchen? Would He be amazed at how much and what you eat?

Remember, He is the King of kings. He is your Savior. Is He your Lord?

Who do you say He is?

Chapter 6

Jesus Christ—His Work

We concluded our look at the Person of Jesus Christ by noting He was both fully God and fully man. He had to be fully God in order to fully guarantee the forgiveness of God and He had to be fully man in order to fully substitute for man. He is indeed God's perfect man and man's perfect God.

The story of Jesus Christ intertwines the person and His work. The Gospel, or Good News, is about who Jesus Christ is *and* what He did.

The Gospel: The Good News.

The apostle Paul wrote out the best and most concise description of this good news in 1 Corinthians 15:1-6.

"Now let me remind you, dear brothers and sisters, of the Good News I preached to you before. You welcomed it then and still do now, for your faith is built on this wonderful message. [2]And it is this Good News that saves you if you firmly believe it—unless, of course, you believed something that was never true in the first place.

[3]"I passed on to you what was most important and what had also been passed on to me—that Christ died for our sins, just as the Scriptures said. [4]He was buried, and he was raised from the dead on the third day, as the Scriptures said. [5]He

was seen by Peter and then by the twelve apostles. ⁶After that, he was seen by more than five hundred of his followers at one time, most of whom are still alive, though some have died by now."

What are the key elements of the good news?

1. "Christ died for our sins." The proof of His death is that He was buried.

   When I was growing up, I thought Jesus died "for" or because of my sins, that somehow, my sins killed Christ. But the Greek wording doesn't give this idea at all. The Greek word translated "for" is *hyper*, which suggests substitution. It means "in place of," "instead of," "on behalf of," or "for the benefit of."

2. "He was raised from the dead." The proof of His resurrection is that He was seen by Peter, the apostles, and hundreds of other people.

   His resurrection appearances prove that He had new life. It all happened according to the Scriptures. This was Jesus, the Son of God, who died for our sins and was raised from the dead to prove He had conquered sin and death.

Another verse provides us with the required response to this good news.

"For God so loved the world that he gave his only Son, so that everyone who believes in him will not perish but have eternal life" (John 3:16).

Our response to the good news of who Jesus is and what He did should be to "believe in Him." The word for "believe" suggests placing your faith in Him, trusting in Him. It is more than intellectual assent.

I believe Queen Elizabeth is the Queen of England but that doesn't make me an Englishman. If I really placed my faith in Queen Elizabeth, perhaps I'd move to London and become a British citizen. The idea of biblical belief is more than intellectual knowledge. It's a matter of trust and faith.

So, you may be saying, "All right. I believe that Jesus Christ is the Son of God. What do I have to believe about His work? What did He actually accomplish?"

Salvation

This chapter deals with the study of salvation or deliverance. From the Greek word *soteria* we have the word *soteriology*, which is the doctrine of salvation. Jesus saves! Let's examine the biblical concept of salvation.

Isaiah 59:2 says, "But there is a problem—your sins have cut you off from God. Because of your sin, he has turned away and will not listen anymore." The New International Version says, "But your iniquities have separated you from your God."

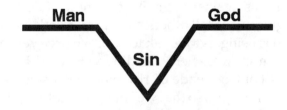

Man is separated from God by sin. We are on one side of a great chasm and God is on the other side. That's the problem.

What is sin? The dictionary defines sin as a transgression of divine law. It's crossing a line God says we are not to cross. It is a trespass beyond a boundary line, a wrong move, a violation of God's law.

The Bible is filled with God's laws, commandments about how we are to live. These are boundary lines for wise living. We can all name some sins. Murder. Lust. Lying. Being disobedient to parents. Pride. All of us are sinners, for as

Romans 3:23 says, "For all have sinned; all fall short of God's glorious standard."

On the other side of the chasm is God. He is pure, holy, totally without sin. Heaven is the perfect dwelling place of God.

As human beings we cannot do anything to bridge the gap between God and ourselves. The solution is that we need to be brought together. We need to be reconciled to God but the Bible clearly teaches that human beings can do nothing to save ourselves. In our hopeless dilemma God comes to our rescue.

Reconciliation

"All this newness of life is from God, who brought us back to himself through what Christ did. And God has given us the task of reconciling people to him. [19]For God was in Christ, reconciling the world to himself, no longer counting people's sins against them. This is the wonderful message he has given us to tell others. [20]We are Christ's ambassadors, and God is using us to speak to you. We urge you, as though Christ himself were here pleading with you, 'Be reconciled to God!' [21]For God made Christ, who never sinned, to be the offering for our sin, so that we could be made right with God through Christ" (2 Corinthians 5:18-21).

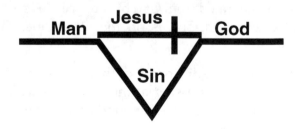

Part of Christ's work is that He reconciled us to God through the cross. He bridged the gap for us. Let's look at this another way.

Bad News and Good News

As Larry Moyer, founder and president of EvanTell, Inc., says, the Bible is filled with bad news and good news. The bad news is about us. The good news is about God. Let's look at both sides in four points.

1. First some of the bad news: "For all have sinned; all fall short of God's glorious standard" (Romans 3:23).

    Sin is described here as falling short—missing the mark or standard of God's absolute perfection. Measured against Him we all fall short. If you and I picked up rocks and tried to throw them to the North Pole we'd both fall short. We tend to measure our selves against other people and sometimes we don't rate too badly. Few of us are mass murderers. Our hope is that God will grade on a curve and we might get into heaven. But that's not what the Bible teaches.

2. The bad news gets worse. "For the wages of sin is death" (Romans 6:23).

    A wage is what we've agreed to work for and what we deserve for our labor. It's what we earned.

    So here we stand, all of us sinners and deserving death for our sins. The Bible talks about that death as eternal separation from God. While we are incapable of doing anything about this problem, God took the initiative and reached down to us. He reconciles us to Himself through Jesus Christ. That's the good news.

3. "But God showed his great love for us by sending Christ to die for us while we were still sinners" (Romans 5:8).

    Imagine that you were in the hospital dying of cancer and I came to visit you with information that medical science had discovered a way to take the cancer cells out of your body and transfer them to someone else. Then I volunteered to have those cancer cells transferred to my body. What would happen to you? Right, you would live. But what would happen to me? Yes, I would die. Well, that's what Christ did. He took our spiritual cancer, our sin, and took the penalty for sin on Himself. He died. But He was more than just another man, so He was raised from death to prove that He had paid the penalty, conquered death, and now offers us new life.

4. The good news continues in Ephesians 2:8-9: "God saved you by his special favor when you believed. And you can't take credit for this; it is a gift from God. ⁹Salvation is not a reward for the good things we have done, so none of us can boast about it."

Grace is a gift. It's free. All you have to do is accept it. You can't do anything to earn a gift. If you pay for a gift, it would no longer be a gift. If someone gives you a gift and you insist on paying for it, the donor would undoubtedly be insulted.

When God offers us salvation as a free gift, why do we try to earn it by our own efforts, thinking that we can be good enough for heaven?

If you're reading this sitting down, think about your chair. You didn't see it manufactured, and you probably didn't test it before sitting down. You just sat down. You trusted it to hold you up. You put your faith in it.[1]

How often have you driven right through a green light without stopping? Think about it. Every time you drive through a green light you're putting your faith in a light covered by a piece of green glass. Actually you're putting your faith in a light covered by a piece of red glass you can't even

---

1.   Copyright, EvanTell, Inc. Used by permission.

see. You're trusting your life to the hope that someone else will see that red light and stop instead of simply driving right into you. How much more can we put our faith into Jesus Christ whom we know is the Son of God?

Do you believe in Christ? Have you accepted His gift of eternal life?

If you don't remember ever trusting Jesus Christ as your personal Savior before today, consider doing it right now. You might want to pray a simple prayer like this to tell God what you're thinking.

"Heavenly Father, I come to you today, knowing that I am a sinner. I believe that Jesus Christ took my place and died on the cross for my sins. Father, please forgive me of my sins. I believe. I'm trusting Jesus Christ as my Savior right now. Thank you for forgiving me and giving me eternal life. Amen."

If you prayed that prayer, you are now a child of God and you will be for all eternity. The fullness of the blessings you have inherited through Jesus Christ will blossom in the days and years ahead as you get to know God better through His Word. We'll be looking at many of these exciting things in the pages ahead.

If you have already trusted Christ as your Savior sometime in the past, or today, you now have two excellent methods by which to share the good news. The "bridge" approach over the chasm of sin has been used by The Navigators for many years. The four verses and illustrations of the "bad news/good news" approach taught by EvanTell is also simple to use. You can underline or color these key verses in your own Bible or use a small tract to show people as you talk with them. You should be able to do at least one of these on a napkin in a restaurant and lead someone to Christ. Pray about it. Study them. Practice.

Reconciliation is part of the saving work of Jesus Christ. What else did He accomplish in this work of salvation?

One of the greatest passages in the Bible is Romans 3:21-25. "But now God has shown us a different way of being right in his sight—not by obeying the law but by the way promised in the Scriptures long ago. [22]We are made right in God's sight when we trust in Jesus Christ to take away our sins. And we all can be saved in this same way, no matter who we are or what we have done.

[23]"For all have sinned; all fall short of God's glorious standard. [24]Yet now God in his gracious kindness declares us **not guilty**. He has done this through Christ Jesus, who has **freed us** by taking away our sins. [25]For God sent Jesus to take the punishment for our sins and **to satisfy God's anger against us. We are made right with God** when we believe that Jesus shed his blood, sacrificing his life for us."

There are three big concepts in this passage we need to examine in some detail so we can understand them more fully.

Justification—Not Guilty

Verse 24 says we are declared "not guilty." Other translations use the term "justified." A legal term used in the first century, it means to be declared righteous or not guilty. Because Christ took our place on the cross when we trust Him to save us, God declares us righteous or not guilty.

Redemption—Set Free

The second concept is also found in verse 24. Jesus Christ "freed us." In describing what happens in our salvation, the apostle Paul now switched to a marketplace term, "redemption." If you have ever returned a soda bottle to get your deposit back, you have "redeemed" it. The term has to do with buying something out of the marketplace never to be bought again, such as a Roman slave set free forever. It carried with it a strong sense of security.

In Hebrews 9:12, the author talked about Christ this way: "Once for all time he took blood into that Most Holy Place, but not the blood of goats and calves. He took his own blood, and with it he secured our salvation forever."

Under the Law of Moses, the high priest of Israel entered the Holy of Holies in the temple and offered up the blood of goats and calves to cover the sins of the people.

The New International Version uses the phrase "having obtained eternal redemption" instead of "secured our salvation forever."

Atonement or Propitiation—To Satisfy God

The third key term in this passage is in verse 25. The New Living Translation says God sent Jesus to satisfy God's anger against us and to make us right with God. The New International Version translates this idea with the theological word "atonement." The New American Standard translates the term "propitiation." It is a theological term.

This concept deals with the Godward aspect of salvation. God is holy and cannot have sin in His presence. Sin provokes the wrath or anger of God. So a penalty must be paid for sin. At the cross Jesus Christ made the payment and God is satisfied. The payment is acceptable. God's holiness and righteousness are satisfied.

In Hebrews 9:5 the same word is used and translated, "the Ark's cover, the place of atonement." It is also called the "mercy seat" or the "atonement cover." This is the covering over the Ark of the Covenant in which were placed the stone tablets on which were written the Ten Commandments. It was located in the Holy of Holies, or Most Holy Place, and is the place where one man, the high priest, could approach and meet the glory of God after sprinkling the blood of the sacrifice on the cover.

These verses in Hebrews help us understand that the whole sacrificial system God dictated to Moses was a foreshadowing of the sacrifice of the Messiah Jesus Christ.

So far we have examined what Christ accomplished on the cross: substitution (He took our place and got what we deserved), reconciliation (we are brought back into a family relationship with God), justification (we are declared "not guilty"), redemption (we are bought at an incredible price, the death of Christ), and propitiation (God's righteousness is satisfied).

But that's not the end of the good news. In fact, it's only half the gospel. Remember 1 Corinthians 15? Christ died (and was buried to prove it). Christ was raised (and seen by over five hundred to prove it). We have been looking at the things Christ accomplished at the cross. What about the rest of the good news?

The Ignored Side of the Gospel

Jesus Christ loved us enough to die for our sins to save us for eternity. He also loved us enough not to leave us the way we were. The first part of the gospel deals with the cross. We are justified and redeemed and God is satisfied with Christ's death in our place as full payment for the death we deserve for our sins. The other part of the gospel centers on the resurrection of Christ and our regeneration—the new life given to us.

When you get a coin in your hand, you get an object with two sides. The sides are inseparable even if you choose to look at only one side. So it is with the gospel. You benefit from all of it, even if you ignore one side.

New Life—Born Again

First Peter 1:3-5 says, "All honor to the God and Father of our Lord Jesus Christ, for it is by his boundless mercy that *God has given us the privilege of being born again. Now we live with a wonderful expectation because Jesus Christ rose again from the dead.* ⁴For God has reserved a priceless inheritance for his children. It is kept in heaven for you, pure and undefiled, beyond the reach of change and decay. ⁵And God, in his mighty power, will protect you until you receive this salvation, because you are trusting him. It will be revealed on the last day for all to see."

The New International Version renders verse 3 this way: "he has given us new birth into a living hope *through the resurrection* of Jesus Christ from the dead."

John 3:3 says, "Jesus replied, 'I assure you, unless you are *born again*, you can never see the Kingdom of God.'"

Titus 3:4-5 says, " But then God our Savior showed us his kindness and love. ⁵He saved us, not because of the good things we did, but because of his mercy. He washed away our sins and gave us a *new life* through the Holy Spirit."

Before salvation we were spiritually dead in our sins. When we trusted Christ, our sins were forgiven **and** we were given new life—new, spiritual life, which lasts forever. We are regenerated or born again through the resurrection.

C. I. Scofield, author of *The Scofield Reference Bible* and former pastor of what is now Scofield Memorial Church in Dallas, Texas, wrote, "It will be seen that regeneration is a creation, not a mere transformation: the bringing in a new thing, not the change of an old. As we received human nature by natural generation, so do we receive the divine nature by regeneration."²

---

2. C. I. Scofield, *Rightly Dividing the Word of Truth*, 1896. (Reprinted by Scripture Truth Book Co. Fincastle, Virginia), p. 47.

Christ Lives In Us

"For this is the secret: *Christ lives in you,* and this is your assurance that you will share in his glory" (Colossians 1:27).

"For when I tried to keep the law, I realized I could never earn God's approval. So I died to the law so that I might live for God. I have been crucified with Christ. [20]I myself no longer live, but *Christ lives in me.* So I live my life in this earthly body by trusting in the Son of God, who loved me and gave himself for me" (Galatians 3:19-20).

"But you are not controlled by your sinful nature. You are controlled by the Spirit if you have the Spirit of God living in you. (And remember that those who do not have the Spirit of Christ living in them are not Christians at all.) [10]Since *Christ lives within you,* even though your body will die because of sin, your spirit is alive because you have been made right with God. [11]The Spirit of God, who raised Jesus from the dead, lives in you. And just as he raised Christ from the dead, he will give life to your mortal body by this same Spirit living within you" (Romans 8:9-11).

Bob George and Tim Stevenson put it this way: "While the message of God's forgiveness through the cross relieves our guilt and gives us assurance of where we will go when we die, it does not give us any power to live here and now. It is through the resurrection of Christ that any man, woman, boy, or girl on the face of the earth who comes to Him in faith receives His very life through the indwelling Holy Spirit! That's how we live!" [3]

Christ Intercedes For Us

"For Christ has entered into heaven itself to appear now before God as our Advocate" (Hebrews 9:24).

---

3. Bob George (and Tim Stevenson), *Classic Christianity (Eugene, Oregon: Harvest House Publishers, 1989), p. 51.*

Christ sits at the right hand of God the Father today interceding for us. He is like our defense attorney. Satan accuses us of unrighteousness in this highest of all courts. Jesus says, "No, this debt was paid in full." And God is satisfied, and so He announces, "Not guilty!"

Eternal Security and Assurance of Salvation

Eternal security and assurance of salvation are two sides of the same coin. Eternal security is what God provides, namely, eternal life. Assurance of salvation is what the believer gets when he accepts the fact of God's security. If you never turned over the coin to see what's there, you might not know.

Some say you can lose your eternal life. But if this were true, how could it be eternal? The Bible is abundantly clear about the eternal security of the believer. Let's look at some of the major passages.

1. "Rejoice because your names are registered as citizens of heaven" (Luke 10:20).

2. "Then he said, 'Jesus, remember me when you come into your Kingdom.' [43]And Jesus replied, 'I assure you, today you will be with me in paradise'" (Luke 23:42-43).

3. "For God so loved the world that he gave his only Son, so that everyone who believes in him will not perish but have eternal life" (John 3:16).

4. "I assure you, those who listen to my message and believe in God who sent me have eternal life. They will never be condemned for their sins, but they have already passed from death into life" (John 5:24).

5. "However, those the Father has given me will come to me, and I will never reject them. [38]For I have come down from heaven to do the will of God who sent me, not to do what I want. [39]And this is the will of

God, that I should not lose even one of all those he has given me, but that I should raise them to eternal life at the last day. [40]For it is my Father's will that all who see his Son and believe in him should have eternal life—that I should raise them at the last day" (John 6:37-40).

6. "My sheep recognize my voice; I know them, and they follow me. [28]I give them eternal life, and they will never perish. No one will snatch them away from me, [29]for my Father has given them to me, and he is more powerful than anyone else. So no one can take them from me. [30]The Father and I are one" (John 10:27-30).

7. "So now there is no condemnation for those who belong to Christ Jesus. [2]For the power of the life-giving Spirit has freed you through Christ Jesus from the power of sin that leads to death" (Romans 8:1-2).

8. "What can we say about such wonderful things as these? If God is for us, who can ever be against us? [32]Since God did not spare even his own Son but gave him up for us all, won't God, who gave us Christ, also give us everything else?

[33]"Who dares accuse us whom God has chosen for his own? Will God? No! He is the one who has given us right standing with himself. [34]Who then will condemn us? Will Christ Jesus? No, for he is the one who died for us and was raised to life for us and is sitting at the place of highest honor next to God, pleading for us.

[35]"Can anything ever separate us from Christ's love? Does it mean he no longer loves us if we have trouble or calamity, or are persecuted, or are hungry or cold or in danger or threatened with death? [36](Even the Scriptures say, 'For your sake we are killed every day; we are being slaughtered like sheep.') [37]No,

despite all these things, overwhelming victory is ours through Christ, who loved us.

[38]"And I am convinced that nothing can ever separate us from his love. Death can't, and life can't. The angels can't, and the demons can't. Our fears for today, our worries about tomorrow, and even the powers of hell can't keep God's love away. [39]Whether we are high above the sky or in the deepest ocean, nothing in all creation will ever be able to separate us from the love of God that is revealed in Christ Jesus our Lord" (Romans 8:31-39).

9. "For we know that when this earthly tent we live in is taken down—when we die and leave these bodies—we will have a home in heaven, an eternal body made for us by God himself and not by human hands. [2]We grow weary in our present bodies, and we long for the day when we will put on our heavenly bodies like new clothing. [3]For we will not be spirits without bodies, but we will put on new heavenly bodies. [4]Our dying bodies make us groan and sigh, but it's not that we want to die and have no bodies at all. We want to slip into our new bodies so that these dying bodies will be swallowed up by everlasting life. [5]God himself has prepared us for this, and as a guarantee he has given us his Holy Spirit" (2 Corinthians 5:1-5).

10. "And now you also have heard the truth, the Good News that God saves you. And when you believed in Christ, he identified you as his own by giving you the Holy Spirit, whom he promised long ago. [14]The Spirit is God's guarantee that he will give us everything he promised and that he has purchased us to be his own people. This is just one more reason for us to praise our glorious God" (Ephesians 1:13-14).

11. "Therefore he is able, once and forever, to save everyone who comes to God through him. He lives

forever to plead with God on their behalf" (Hebrews 7:25).

12. "All honor to the God and Father of our Lord Jesus Christ, for it is by his boundless mercy that God has given us the privilege of being born again. Now we live with a wonderful expectation because Jesus Christ rose again from the dead. ⁴For God has reserved a priceless inheritance for his children. It is kept in heaven for you, pure and undefiled, beyond the reach of change and decay. ⁵And God, in his mighty power, will protect you until you receive this salvation, because you are trusting him. It will be revealed on the last day for all to see" (1 Peter 1:3-5).

If you have trusted Christ as your Savior, your place in heaven is secure by the promise and power of God. God did it all. Your eternal security depends on Him, not you. If you do believe God's promises, you can also have assurance of your eternal salvation.

Knowing for Sure

First John 5:13 is the greatest Bible passage on the assurance of salvation. John wrote, "I write this to you who believe in the Son of God, so that you may *know* you have eternal life."

It does not say "hope," "pray," "feel," "think," or any other such word. God wants us to *KNOW* we have eternal life.

Why do some true believers not understand this? Some may never have heard the teaching of eternal security systematically taught. I have had the privilege of teaching at a pastoral conference in the rural mountains of Kenya, Africa. The pastors were godly people, but some had little formal training in theology. Their denomination had been founded a century ago by missionaries who did not believe in assurance of salvation. Few of these pastors owned any books except a Bible and a song book in their native dialect. One elderly pastor, in his seventies, prayed at the start of the week that he would endure and safely pass through this life so that he would get to heaven. This godly old man did not know for sure whether he would get to heaven. It broke my heart. Later that week, when I had finished teaching on eternal security and the assurance of salvation, he came up to me and embraced me. He and hundreds of other church leaders knew for sure they were going to heaven. What a blessing! God wants us to know!

Others have heard and read the above-cited key passages in the Bible, but they refuse to believe God's Word.

Some people have false concepts about eternal security. They may be depending on their "feelings" rather than on the clear truth of God's Word.

Other people may not be walking in obedience to God and so they feel He is far from them. The lack of intimate fellowship with God would tend to make a believer "feel" unsure of his or her eternal destiny. Walking in obedient dependence on Him, yielding our lives to the Spirit of Christ "in us," produces confidence and assurance.

Practical Life Application

What does the work of Christ mean to us today?

If you've never trusted Christ as your Savior, this is the time to do it.

If you've never learned a method of explaining the good news to someone, you now are equipped to share both the "bridge" explanation and the "bad news/good news" method. Obtain tracts and other materials from evangelistic organizations like The Navigators, EvanTell, Stonecroft, The American Tract Society, or Campus Crusade for Christ. Pray and practice.

You know you have eternal life. Nothing can ever change that. You know how the story ends. Live like it. Be all that God wants you to be.

Many Christians through the centuries have never fully understood the life of Christ in them. Don't ignore the other side of the good news, the power of the resurrected life you now have in Christ.

Major Ian Thomas put it this way: "Christ gave His life for us, to give new life to us, so He could live His life through us." [4]

---

4.   Major Ian Thomas, Winter Bible Conference, (Lewisville, Texas, Crossroads Bible Church, 1996).

Chapter 7

The Holy Spirit

In chapter four we saw that the Holy Spirit is God, who proceeds (as to His role, not creation) from the Father and the Son. He is referred to as the third person of the Trinity. He seems to act as an agent of the Father and the Son, rather than for Himself. This may be why it took the church several hundred years to fully recognize the personhood of the Holy Spirit. (As noted earlier in the Creed of Constantinople, A.D. 381: "We believe in the Holy Spirit, the Lord and life-giver, Who proceeds from the Father [and the Son], Who is worshipped and glorified together with the Father and the Son, Who spoke through the prophets." The Holy Spirit is a person, not an abstract force from a Star Wars' script. The Holy Spirit is presented in Scripture as regenerating, indwelling, baptizing, energizing, and sanctifying.

His Person

The Holy Spirit is called God. In Acts 5:3-4, a man and his wife were caught deceiving the church on a matter of money. "Then Peter said, 'Ananias, why has Satan filled your heart? *You lied to the Holy Spirit*, and you kept some of the money for yourself. *The property was yours to sell or not sell, as you wished. And after selling it, the money was yours to give away. How could you do a thing like this? *You* *weren't lying to us but to God."* Notice that their lie was to the Holy Spirit, who later is called God.

He Has the Attributes of God

The Bible also talks about the Holy Spirit having the attributes of God.

He is eternal. The Holy Spirit is seen in the creation story, indicating that He is eternal. "In the beginning God created the heavens and the earth. The earth was empty, a formless mass cloaked in darkness. And the Spirit of God was hovering over its surface. Then God said, 'Let there be light,' and there was light" (Gen. 1:1-3).

He is all-powerful (omnipotent). "His [God's] Spirit made the heavens beautiful, and his power pierced the gliding serpent. These are some of the minor things he does, merely a whisper of his power. Who can understand the thunder of his power?" (Job 26:13-14).

He is all-knowing (omniscient). "That is what the Scriptures mean when they say, 'No eye has seen, no ear has heard, and no mind has imagined what God has prepared for those who love him.' [10]But we know these things because God has revealed them to us by his Spirit, and his Spirit searches out everything and shows us even God's deep secrets. [11]No one can know what anyone else is really thinking except that person alone, and no one can know God's thoughts except God's own Spirit" (1 Corinthians 2:9-11).

He Performs the Work of God

Elihu said, "For the Spirit of God has made me, and the breath of the Almighty gives me life" (Job 33:4).

"When you send your Spirit, new life is born to replenish all the living of the earth" (Psalm 104:30).

The Holy Spirit Is the Object of Faith

"Do not banish me from your presence, and don't take your Holy Spirit from me" (Psalm 51:11).

"Jesus commanded, 'Therefore, go and make disciples of all the nations, baptizing them in the name of the Father and the Son and the Holy Spirit'" (Matthew 28:19).

The apostle Peter took orders from God the Holy Spirit in reaching out to Gentiles, starting with the house of Cornelius. "Meanwhile, as Peter was puzzling over the vision, the Holy Spirit said to him, 'three men have come looking for you. ²⁰Go down and go with them without hesitation. All is well, for I have sent them'" (Acts 10:19-20).

The Work of the Holy Spirit in the Old Testament

Creation. We've already noted the Spirit's participation in the creation of the world as described in Genesis 1:2.

Prophecy. "'Stand up, son of man,' said the voice. 'I want to speak with you.' ²The Spirit came into me as he spoke and set me on my feet. I listened carefully to his words. ³'Son of man,' he said, 'I am sending you to the nation of Israel, a nation that is rebelling against me. Their ancestors have rebelled against me from the beginning, and they are still in revolt to this very day. ⁴They are a hard-hearted and stubborn people. But I am sending you to say to them, "this is what the Sovereign LORD says!" ⁵And whether they listen or not—for remember, they are rebels—at least they will know they have had a prophet among them'" (Ezekiel 2:1-5).

Equipping. God equipped special people to build the tabernacle.

"The LORD also said to Moses, ²'Look, I have chosen Bezalel son of Uri, grandson of Hur, of the tribe of Judah. ³*I have filled him with the Spirit of God*, giving him great wisdom, intelligence, and skill in all kinds of crafts. ⁴He is able to create beautiful objects from gold, silver, and bronze. ⁵He is skilled in cutting and setting gemstones and in carving wood. Yes, he is a master at every craft!'" (Exodus 31:1-5).

Administration. Joseph was made ruler of Egypt when even the Pharaoh recognized his unique blessing through the power of the Holy Spirit. "As they discussed who should be appointed for the job, Pharaoh said, 'Who could do it better than Joseph? *For he is a man who is obviously filled with the spirit of God*'" (Genesis 41:38).

In the wilderness God put His Spirit on the seventy elders to help Moses administer the nation of Israel (Numbers 11:16-17). In Deuteronomy 34:9, Joshua was called to replace Moses, and Joshua was *"full of the spirit of wisdom."*

Instruction for the Spiritual Life. *"'You sent your good Spirit to instruct them,'* said the prophet Nehemiah'" (Nehemiah 9:20).

"Teach me to do your will, for you are my God. *May your gracious Spirit lead me forward* on a firm footing" (Psalm 143:10).

The Work of the Holy Spirit in the Life of Christ

With Mary. "Mary asked the angel, 'But how can I have a baby? I am a virgin.' [35]The angel replied, 'The Holy Spirit will come upon you, and the power of the Most High will overshadow you. So the baby born to you will be holy, and he will be called the Son of God'" (Luke 1:35).

With John the Baptist. "One day when the crowds were being baptized, Jesus himself was baptized. As he was praying, the heavens opened, [22]and the Holy Spirit descended on him in the form of a dove. And a voice from heaven said, 'You are my beloved Son, and I am fully pleased with you'" (Luke 3:21-22).

At the Cross. "For by the power of the eternal Spirit, Christ offered himself to God as a perfect sacrifice for our sins" (Hebrews 9:14).

Christ lived His earthly life in the power of the Holy Spirit, yielding to the guidance of the Spirit and the will of God the Father.

The Work of the Holy Spirit Today

He convicts. "But now I am going away to the one who sent me, and none of you has asked me where I am going. [6]Instead, you are very sad. [7]But it is actually best for you that I go away, because if I don't, the Counselor won't come. If I do go away, he will come because I will send him to you. [8]And when he comes, he will convince the world of its sin, and of God's righteousness, and of the coming judgment. [9]The world's sin is unbelief in me" (John 16:5-9).

He teaches. "When the Spirit of truth comes, he will guide you into all truth. He will not be presenting his own ideas; he will be telling you what he has heard. He will tell you about the future. [14]He will bring me glory by revealing to you whatever he receives from me. [15]All that the Father has is mine; this is what I mean when I say that the Spirit will reveal to you whatever he receives from me" (John 16:13-15).

"But when the Father sends the Counselor as my representative—and by the Counselor I mean the Holy Spirit—he will teach you everything and will remind you of everything I myself have told you" (John 14:26).

"But we know these things because God has revealed them to us by his Spirit, and his Spirit searches out everything and shows us even God's deep secrets. [11]No one can know what anyone else is really thinking except that person alone, and no one can know God's thoughts except God's own Spirit. [12]And God has actually given us his Spirit (not the world's spirit) so we can know the wonderful things God has freely given us. [13]When we tell you this, we do not use words of human wisdom. We speak words given to us by the Spirit, using the Spirit's words to explain spiritual truths. [14]But people who aren't Christians can't understand these truths from God's Spirit. It all sounds foolish to them because only those who have the Spirit can understand what the Spirit means. [15]We who have the Spirit understand these things, but others can't understand us at all. [16]How could they? For, 'Who can know what the LORD is thinking? Who can give him counsel?' But we can understand these things, for we have the mind of Christ" (1 Corinthians 2:10-16).

He intercedes. "And the Holy Spirit helps us in our distress. For we don't even know what we should pray for, nor how we should pray. But the Holy Spirit prays for us with groanings that cannot be expressed in words. [27]And the Father who knows all hearts knows what the Spirit is saying, for the Spirit pleads for us believers in harmony with God's own will. [28]And we know that God causes everything to work together for the good of those who love God and are called according to his purpose for them" (Romans 8:26-28).

He appoints to special service. "One day as these men were worshipping the Lord and fasting, the Holy Spirit said, 'Dedicate Barnabas and Saul for the special work I have for them'" (Acts 13:2).

The Holy Spirit is engaged in five other major works today that deserve more detailed attention.

Regeneration

People are regenerated by the Holy Spirit when they place their faith and trust in Christ.

"Jesus replied, 'I assure you, unless you are born again, you can never see the Kingdom of God.'

[4]"What do you mean?' exclaimed Nicodemus. 'How can an old man go back into his mother's womb and be born again?'

[5]"Jesus replied, 'The truth is, no one can enter the Kingdom of God without being born of water and the Spirit. [6]Humans can reproduce only human life, but *the Holy Spirit gives new life from heaven*'" (John 3:3-6).

"But then God our Savior showed us his kindness and love. ⁵He saved us, not because of the good things we did, but because of his mercy. He washed away our sins and *gave us a new life through the Holy Spirit.* ⁶He generously poured out the Spirit upon us because of what Jesus Christ our Savior did. ⁷He declared us not guilty because of his great kindness. And now we know that we will inherit eternal life" (Titus 3:4-7).

Indwelling

Hundreds of years before Christ the prophets told about a new promise, a new covenant between God and His people.

"And I will give you a new heart with new and right desires, and I will put a new spirit in you. I will take out your stony heart of sin and give you a new, obedient heart. ²⁷And *I will put my Spirit in you* so you will obey my laws and do whatever I command" (Ezekiel 36:26-27).

"'The day will come,' says the LORD, 'when I will make a new covenant with the people of Israel and Judah. ³²This covenant will not be like the one I made with their ancestors when I took them by the hand and brought them out of the land of Egypt. They broke that covenant, though I loved them as a husband loves his wife,' says the LORD.

³³"'But this is the new covenant I will make with the people of Israel on that day,' says the LORD. 'I will put my laws in their minds, and I will write them on their hearts. I will be their God, and they will be my people'" (Jeremiah 31:31-33).

While these promises were for Israel, and the church today is not Israel, God gives believers today the blessing of the indwelling Holy Spirit. One day these promises of the New Covenant will be totally fulfilled in Israel.

In Old Testament accounts the Holy Spirit came upon people for a time, a special anointing or power given for special service. In the New Testament or Church Age all believers are indwelt by the Holy Spirit, promised as part of the New Covenant, which Christ proclaimed at the Last Supper.

"Or don't you know that *your body is the temple of the Holy Spirit, who lives in you* and was given to you by God? You do not belong to yourself, [20]for God bought you with a high price. So you must honor God with your body" (1 Corinthians 6:19-20).

Now that the Holy Spirit indwells all believers, it follows that He also is present in the church, both universal and local, where believers gather together.

"Don't you realize that all of you together are the temple of God and that the Spirit of God lives in you? [17]God will bring ruin upon anyone who ruins this temple. For God's temple is holy, and you Christians are that temple" (1 Corinthians 3:16-17).

We have the ongoing power of God the Holy Spirit in us to enable us to have Christ live His life through us. The indwelling of the Holy Spirit is not simply an experience. It is a fact.

Sealing by the Holy Spirit

The Spirit's ministry in sealing us is also not just a feeling or experience. It, too, is a fact documented by Scripture.

The concept of sealing comes from ancient days when kings wore signet rings with their own personal seal engraved on the ring. When they sent official proclamations, their correspondence was closed or sealed with hot wax and imprinted by the king's unique ring to show that the message was official and authentic. The seal was not questioned. It was the king's identification and guarantee.

"And now you also have heard the truth, the Good News that God saves you. And when you believed in Christ, he identified you as his own by giving you the Holy Spirit, whom he promised long ago. [14]The Spirit is God's guarantee that he will give us everything he promised and that he has purchased us to be his own people. This is just one more reason for us to praise our glorious God" (Ephesians 1:13-14).

In verse 13 the New International Version uses the phrase "Having believed, you were marked in him with a seal."

Baptized by the Spirit

After His resurrection Jesus told his apostles, "John (the Baptist) baptized with water, but in just a few days you will be baptized with the Holy Spirit" (Acts. 1:5). Days later, as described in Acts 2, this happened when "everyone present was filled with the Holy Spirit." In Peter's speech, he talked about the prophet Joel's prediction that "in the last days, God said, 'I will pour out my Spirit upon all people'" (Acts 2:17).

As Peter went on talking about Jesus, he said, "And the Father, as he had promised, gave him the Holy Spirit to pour out on us, just as you see and hear today" (Acts 2:33).

The word *baptism* comes from the Greek, *baptizo*, used in the first century for dyeing cloth. When a color dye is added to water and material is dipped into it, the fabric changes color and becomes identified with the new color instead of its previous natural shade. When believers are "baptized" into Christ, they are identified with Him.

Water baptism is a picture of what happens when we trust Christ. It is a public identification with Christ.

Spirit baptism happens to all believers at the moment of salvation. When the Holy Spirit came on the disciples on the Day of Pentecost in Acts 2, no water was involved. The pouring of the Spirit on believers is a fact, remembered, portrayed, and dramatized by water baptism later in response to Christ's command. Just as we remember Christ's death, His body and blood given for us, in the Lord's Supper, so we remember His resurrection and the baptism, or identification with His Spirit, in water baptism.

Some people believe that Spirit baptism occurs sometimes after salvation and is a so-called "second blessing." Many believe it is accompanied by the ability to do miracles such as speaking in languages not previously known, as the apostles were able to do. In the early days of the church many were able to perform miracles, but always as an authenticating ministry to verify their authority in preaching the truth about Christ. Once the church was established and the entire New Testament written, before the end of the first century, there was no longer a need for these authenticating or sign gifts, and they disappeared as the norm for Christians.

Christians are baptized in the Spirit at salvation, as seen in this verse: "Some of us are Jews, some are Gentiles, some are slaves, and some are free. But *we have all been baptized into Christ's body by one Spirit, and we have all received the same Spirit*" (1 Corinthians 12:13).

"*All*" not some. Not just the spiritually mature. Not just people saved for more than a year, or a month, or a week. Not just people who believe they have the "gift of tongues." "All" includes even someone who trusted Christ five seconds ago. Or a believer who has fallen back into a life of sin.

Nowhere in Scripture is anyone told to be baptized by the Spirit. We are urged, however, to be filled with the Spirit.

The Filling of the Spirit

Some people think the filling of the Spirit has to do with our getting more of the Holy Spirit. A better way to look at this is that the Spirit gets more of us. To be filled with the Spirit is to be controlled by the Spirit.

"So be careful how you live, not as fools but as those who are wise. [16]Make the most of every opportunity for doing good in these evil days. [17]Don't act thoughtlessly, but try to understand what the LORD wants you to do. [18]Don't be drunk with wine, because that will ruin your life. Instead, *let the Holy Spirit fill and control you.* [19]Then you will sing psalms and hymns and spiritual songs among yourselves, making music to the LORD in your hearts. [20]And you will always give thanks for everything to God the Father in the name of our LORD Jesus Christ" (Ephesians 5:15-20).

But how can we let the Holy Spirit fill and control us?

Let's look at a companion verse, also written by the apostle Paul.

"Let the words of Christ, in all their richness, live in your hearts and make you wise. Use his words to teach and counsel each other. Sing psalms and hymns and spiritual songs to God with thankful hearts. [17]And whatever you do or say, let it be as a representative of the Lord Jesus, all the while giving thanks through him to God the Father" (Colossians 3:16-17).

Both passages conclude the same way. They both talk about encouraging relationships, having joy with a melody in your heart (emotional well-being), giving thanks and being grateful to God in the name of Christ.

In the first passage, from Ephesians 5, this kind of joyful life is the result of being filled with the Spirit. In the second passage, from Colossians 3, this joyful life is the result of being filled with the "words of Christ," letting them dwell in us.

Where do we find the words of Christ? In the Bible, of course. We'll examine some practical steps shortly but first we need to look at some related ideas.

Filling and Maturity

Being filled or controlled by the Holy Spirit is not the same as being spiritually mature. Even newborn baby Christians can be filled with the Spirit. Many of us probably can relate to this. In the first few weeks or months after trusting Christ we are "on fire" spiritually. We're enthusiastic about our faith. We may not know a lot abut our salvation, but what we do know we like, so we stay in fellowship and prayer and keep learning. It feels great to feel close to God and we like it. It's a great experience.

Then perhaps our circumstances change. We may have been filled with the Spirit soon after our conversion, but because we were not mature Christians we may have lost our enthusiasm. We may let our human circumstances in our fallen world rob us of that experience of joy. Sometimes it's our sin that does it—our desires, based on old thinking and experiences, that something apart from God Himself can make us happy and fulfilled.

So while we can never lose the indwelling Holy Spirit Himself, we lose the experience of His filling us, His control of our lives, by taking back control ourselves in some areas.

Christian maturity comes with growth. As we grow in Christ, we are encouraged to live continually under the control of the Spirit, to always be filled with the Spirit, and to experience the joy that comes from His filling.

Practical Life Application

So how do we grow in Christ? How do we become more mature as Christians? How can we be filled with the *Spirit* of God? By being filled with the *Word* of God.

We need to stay in the Word of God—hearing, reading, studying, meditating, memorizing the Bible. That's the major way, as suggested by those parallel passages in Ephesians 5 and Colossians 3. But there are other suggestions.

What Not to Do

Let's look at two negative approaches, things we are told *not to do.*

First Thessalonians 5:19 says, *"Do not stifle the Holy Spirit."* The New International Version says, "Do not put out the Spirit's fire;" The King James Version translates this, "Do not quench the Spirit."

This means saying no to the Spirit's leading. "My will be done, not Yours."

We are to yield our will in favor of God's will, to make His way of thinking our way of thinking.

In Romans 12:1-2, Paul wrote, "And so, dear brothers and sisters, I plead with you to give your bodies to God. Let them be a living and holy sacrifice—the kind he will accept. When you think of what he has done for you, is this too much to ask? [2]Don't copy the behavior and customs of this world, but *let God transform you into a new person by changing the way you think.* Then you will know what God wants you to do, and you will know how good and pleasing and perfect his will really is."

Another thing we are told *not to do* is in Ephesians 4:30. Here we are also told *not to "bring sorrow to God's Holy Spirit."*

"And do not bring sorrow to God's Holy Spirit by the way you live. Remember, he is the one who has identified you as his own, guaranteeing that you will be saved on the day of redemption. [31]Get rid of all bitterness, rage, anger, harsh words, and slander, as well as all types of malicious behavior. [32]Instead, be kind to each other, tenderhearted, forgiving one another, just as God through Christ has forgiven you. Follow God's example in everything you do, because you are his dear children. [2]Live a life filled with love for others, following the example of Christ, who loved you and gave himself as a sacrifice to take away your sins. And God was pleased, because that sacrifice was like sweet perfume to him. [3]Let there be no sexual immorality, impurity, or greed among you. Such sins have no place among God's people. [4]Obscene stories, foolish talk, and coarse

jokes—these are not for you. Instead, let there be thankfulness to God" (Ephesians 4:30-5:4).

Bringing sorrow to the Holy Spirit refers to continuous,
sinful, disobedience to God. If you are a Christian, you
ought not be sexually immoral, greedy, obscene, angry, bitter, or unforgiving. Christians make mistakes and sin, but
continually living such a lifestyle grieves the Holy Spirit,
who lives in you.

If this kind of lifestyle dominates or is in the life of a believer, there is a need for repentance, a turning from those
ways, and turning back toward God and His will for your
life.

What to Do

We are also given a positive way of being filled with the
Spirit in Galatians 5:16-17: "So I advise you *to live according to
your new life in the Holy Spirit*. Then you won't be doing what
your sinful nature craves. [17]The old sinful nature loves to do
evil, which is just opposite from what the Holy Spirit wants.
And the Spirit gives us desires that are opposite from what
the sinful nature desires. These two forces are constantly
fighting each other, and your choices are never free from
this conflict."

The Greek word translated "live" here is *peripateo*. It has
also been translated *"walk in the Spirit"* or *"walk by the Spirit."*

Walking in the Spirit gives us a beautiful picture. It's not
run or fly. When you walk, you take one step at a time. It's a
process.

Can a baby walk? Not right away. But somewhere
around nine months to a year old a baby begins to walk.
When he or she falls, we don't yell, "You're hopeless!
You'll never walk!" Of course not. We encourage the baby to
keep trying, to take one step at a time until walking becomes
second nature to it. It's the same with spiritual walking. We
have a new nature and we have to learn to walk in the Spirit,

one step at a time, until walking in obedience to the Holy Spirit's leading is a natural process.

Where do we learn what it is we are to obey? In the Bible. So we need to listen to it, read it, study it, meditate on it, memorize it. Think about how to apply what you learn to your life.

How do we know when we are in step with the Holy Spirit? What should be evident in the life of a Christian who is walking in the Spirit?

The "fruit of the Spirit!" "But when the Holy Spirit controls our lives, he will produce this kind of fruit in us: love, joy, peace, patience, kindness, goodness, faithfulness, [23]gentleness, and self-control. Here there is no conflict with the law. [24]Those who belong to Christ Jesus have nailed the passions and desires of their sinful nature to his cross and crucified them there. [25]If we are living now by the Holy Spirit, let us follow the Holy Spirit's leading in every part of our lives" (Galatians 5:22-25).

The Spirit Is Our Internal Air Traffic Controller

Do you know what it's like to approach a fogged-in airport with less fuel then you need to be able to go anywhere but on the runway, a runway you can't even see?

Mature pilots know their flight manual. They know their airplane. They know the instrument panel. In the same way we need to know the Bible. We also need to understand ourselves and our circumstances from God's perspective, not just our own.

I've heard Neal Anderson illustrate it this way. Just as pilots, who have landed their planes hundreds of times, have confidence based on their experience, Christians will have confidence from every step of faith we've taken in the past, no matter how ominous the storm over the runway we're facing. But we're not relying on a formula, a program, or even a Bible verse we memorized. The air traffic controller will talk the pilot down to safety. So too the Holy Spirit is a person who seals you in Christ forever. We can trust the Spirit of God. We can learn to walk in Him in faith because the Holy Spirit lives in us and talks with us. He's our own internal air traffic controller.[1]

Listen to Him. Learn to rely on Him. Depend on Him, instead of depending on yourself.

Is there any part of your life you're holding back from God? What part do you refuse to give to the Holy Spirit's control? Your career? Your money? Your children? Your hobbies? Your relationships? Your anger? Your TV? Your fantasies?

Evaluate your life in light of the nine evidences of the fruit. Is one of the nine characteristics missing in your life? What can you do to cultivate that quality?

Are you "stifling the Spirit" by saying no? Then give up. Surrender your will to His. Say "Yes, Lord!"

Are you "bringing sorrow to God's Spirit" by sinning over and over? Then turn from it. If it's too big a problem, get help.

Are you walking in the Spirit, that is, walking in faith, trusting God to deliver you even if you're afraid? Take a baby step. And then another. It gets easier with each step. Learn to walk in the Spirit.

(One other aspect of the ministry of the Holy Spirit involves spiritual gifts. We'll examine this subject in Chapter 10, The Church.)

---

1. Neil Anderson, *Walking in the Light* (Nashville: Thomas Nelson Publishers, 1992), pp. 173-174.

Chapter 8

Looking at the World from God's Point of View

From the time you were born until your parents die, they probably dealt with you in different ways, depending on how old you were, how mature you were, and so forth. If you have children, you have or will relate to them in different ways over time. We usually don't treat a six-month-old the way we treat a twenty-six-year-old. There are different purposes and different responsibilities at different times.

God, our heavenly Father, is the same. In the biblical record, there are different periods of time or ages in which God has dispensed different responsibilities to people. Theologians call these times "dispensations."

What Is a "Dispensation"?

A dispensation is a period of time, an age, or an economy in which God has given man distinctive responsibilities. These are rules for the administration of life, according to God's unfolding and progressive revelation to that point in history.

Let's look at Galatians 1:3-5: "May grace and peace be yours from God our Father and from the Lord Jesus Christ.

[4]He died for our sins, just as God our Father planned, in order to rescue us from this evil world in which we live. [5]That is why all glory belongs to God *through all the ages of eternity.* Amen."

In Colossians 1:25, Paul wrote about his God-given responsibility. "God has given me the responsibility of serving his church by proclaiming his message in all its fullness to you Gentiles." The message revealed to Paul, kept secret before then, was that God now lives in believers. "Christ lives in you" (v. 27), and Gentiles share in His glory.

Another key passage is Ephesians 3:1-11. "I, Paul, am a prisoner of Christ Jesus because of my preaching to you Gentiles. [2]As you already know, God has given me this special ministry of announcing his favor to you Gentiles. [3]As I briefly mentioned earlier in this letter, God himself revealed his secret plan to me. [4]As you read what I have written, you will understand what I know about this plan regarding Christ. [5]God did not reveal it to previous generations, but now he has revealed it by the Holy Spirit to his holy apostles and prophets.

[6]"And this is the secret plan: The Gentiles have an equal share with the Jews in all the riches inherited by God's children. Both groups have believed the Good News, and both are part of the same body and enjoy together the promise of blessings through Christ Jesus. [7]By God's special favor and mighty power, I have been given the wonderful privilege of serving him by spreading this Good News.

[8]"Just think! Though I did nothing to deserve it, and though I am the least deserving Christian there is, I was chosen for this special joy of telling the Gentiles about the endless treasures available to them in Christ. [9]I was chosen to explain to everyone this plan that God, the Creator of all things, had kept secret from the beginning.

[10]"God's purpose was to show his wisdom in all its rich variety to all the rulers and authorities in the heavenly

realms. They will see this when Jews and Gentiles are joined together in his church. "This was his plan from all eternity, and it has now been carried out through Christ Jesus our Lord" (Ephesians 3:1-11).

In *Major Bible Themes* Lewis Sperry Chafer and John F. Walvoord wrote, "It is probable that the recognition of the dispensations sheds more light on the whole message of the Bible than any other aspect of biblical study. Often the first clear understanding of the dispensations and God's revealed purposes in them results in the beginning of useful Bible knowledge and in the fostering of a personal interest in the Bible itself."[1]

The key to understanding these various dispensations is how you interpret the Bible. A literal, or normal, plain interpretation, followed consistently throughout the Bible, will lead you to be a dispensationalist.

Seven major dispensations, or times, are revealed in the Bible. Each is distinguished by three characteristics: The revelation of how God rules at that time, man's relationship to God at that time, and man's responsibilities at that time.

Let's examine each of the seven dispensations as we take a broad look at world history from God's point of view.

The Seven Dispensations

1. Dispensation of Innocence

Adam and Eve in the garden. (Genesis 1:26–3:6)

2. Dispensation of Conscience

From the Fall to the Flood. (Genesis 3:7–8:19)

---

1 Louis Sperry Chafer and John F. Walvoord. *Major Bible Themes* (Grand Rapids: Zondervan Publishing House, 1974) pps. 126-127.

3. **Dispensation of Human Government**

   Noah to the Tower of Babel. (Genesis 8:20–11:9)

4. **Dispensation of Promise**

   From Abraham to Israel's slavery in Egypt. (Genesis 11:10–Exodus 19:2)

5. **Dispensation of Law**

   From Moses to Jesus Christ. (Exodus 19:3–Acts 1:26)

6. **Dispensation of Grace ***

   From Pentecost to the rapture of the church. (See Ephesians 3:1-10. The rapture is described in 1 Thessalonians 4:16 & 17. Scriptures concerning the Age of Grace include John 13-17; Acts 1 through Revelation 3. See also Jeremiah 31:31 and Ezekiel 36:27.)

   Interlude: The Tribulation on Earth
   (Rev. 6; 8; 9-14; 16-18; 19:11-21)

   Bema Seat and Wedding Feast in Heaven
   (2 Cor. 5:10-11; Rev. 19:7-9)

7. **Dispensation of the Kingdom**

   Jesus Christ rules the world from David's throne in Jerusalem. (Psalm 72; Isaiah 2:1-5;   9:6 -7; 11;   Jeremiah 33:14-17; Daniel 2:44-45; 7:9-14, 18, 27; Matthew 24; Luke 1:31-33; Revelation 19-20).

   Eternity: The White Throne Judgment and
   the New Jerusalem and the New Earth
   (Revelation 20:11–22:21)

   * Note: The most common way to group the dispensations is to show the period of grace, our present age, as an interlude occurring in the Dispensation of Law, which was interrupted by Christ's founding of His church. After the rapture of the church, an attempt will be made to institute the Law again by Israel during the seven-year Tribulation.

A Closer Look at Each Dispensation

Let's look at each dispensation according to man's responsibilities, his failures, and the resulting judgment.

1. Dispensation of Innocence.

"Then God said, 'Let us make people in our image, to be like ourselves. They will be masters over all life—the fish in the sea, the birds in the sky, and all the livestock, wild animals, and small animals.'

[27]"So God created people in his own image; God patterned them after himself; male and female he created them.

[28]"God blessed them and told them, 'Multiply and fill the earth and subdue it. Be masters over the fish and birds and all the animals.' [29]And God said, 'Look! I have given you the seed-bearing plants throughout the earth and all the fruit trees for your food. [30]And I have given all the grasses and other green plants to the animals and birds for their food.' And so it was. [31]Then God looked over all he had made, and he saw that it was excellent in every way. This all happened on the sixth day" (Genesis 1:26-31).

"The LORD God placed the man in the Garden of Eden to tend and care for it. [16]But the LORD God gave him this warning: 'You may freely eat any fruit in the garden [17]except fruit from the tree of the knowledge of good and evil. If you eat of its fruit, you will surely die'" (Genesis 2:15-17).

What were man's responsibilities? Mankind was to be master over all other life and to have children and rule over the earth. Everything was made for mankind's rule and care as stewards under God. They had everything they needed. There was only one prohibition: not to eat fruit from the one tree of good and evil.

Man's failure is recorded in Genesis 3:1-6. "Now the serpent was the shrewdest of all the creatures the LORD God had made. 'Really?' he asked the woman. 'Did God really say you must not eat any of the fruit in the garden?'

²"'Of course we may eat it,' the woman told him. ³'It's only the fruit from the tree at the center of the garden that we are not allowed to eat. God says we must not eat it or even touch it, or we will die.'

⁴"'You won't die!' the serpent hissed. ⁵'God knows that your eyes will be opened when you eat it. You will become just like God, knowing everything, both good and evil.'

⁶"'The woman was convinced. The fruit looked so fresh and delicious, and it would make her so wise! So she ate some of the fruit. She also gave some to her husband, who was with her. Then he ate it, too" (Genesis 3:1-6).

Adam and Eve had everything going for them, and yet they blew it! Given a choice, they chose to disobey God.

What was the resulting judgment? Everything changed. Adam and Eve feared God. They were banished from the Garden. Death entered the world as God sacrificed animals for skins to cover them. They lost their close, intimate fellowship with God.

2. Dispensation of Conscience.

"At that moment, their eyes were opened, and they suddenly felt shame at their nakedness. So they strung fig leaves together around their hips to cover themselves.

⁸"Toward evening they heard the LORD God walking about in the garden, so they hid themselves among the trees. ⁹The LORD God called to Adam, 'Where are you?'

¹⁰"He replied, 'I heard you, so I hid. I was afraid because I was naked.'

¹¹"'Who told you that you were naked?' the LORD God asked. 'Have you eaten the fruit I commanded you not to eat?'

¹²"'Yes,' Adam admitted, 'but it was the woman you gave me who brought me the fruit, and I ate it.'

¹³"Then the LORD God asked the woman, 'How could you do such a thing?' 'The serpent tricked me,' she replied. 'That's why I ate it.'

¹⁴"So the LORD God said to the serpent, 'Because you have done this, you will be punished. You are singled out from all the domestic and wild animals of the whole earth to be cursed. You will grovel in the dust as long as you live, crawling along on your belly. ¹⁵From now on, you and the woman will be enemies, and your offspring and her off-spring will be enemies. He will crush your head, and you will strike his heel.'

¹⁶"Then he said to the woman, 'You will bear children with intense pain and suffering. And though your desire will be for your husband, he will be your master.' ¹⁷And to Adam he said, 'Because you listened to your wife and ate the fruit I told you not to eat, I have placed a curse on the ground. All your life you will struggle to scratch a living from it. ¹⁸It will grow thorns and thistles for you, though you will eat of its grains. ¹⁹All your life you will sweat to produce food, until your dying day. Then you will return to the ground from which you came. For you were made from dust, and to the dust you will return'" (Genesis 3:7-19).

Adam and Eve were then banished from the garden. Man was now to live according to the knowledge of good and evil, according to his own conscience.

What was cursed as a result of man's sin? Satan. Eve's seed (Christ) would one day crush Satan's head. This is the earliest prophetic comment on the Savior to come. Adam and Eve were also cursed by their new sin nature. And the whole earth was cursed.

But could man live a godly life by following his con-science? We see the answer in Genesis 4 when Adam and Eve's son Cain murdered his brother Abel. The wickedness of the human heart dominated man's society at the time of Noah.

"Now the LORD observed the extent of the people's wickedness, and he saw that all their thoughts were consistently and totally evil. ⁶So the LORD was sorry he had ever made them. It broke his heart. ⁷And the LORD said, 'I will completely wipe out this human race that I have created. Yes, and I will destroy all the animals and birds, too. I am sorry I ever made them.' ⁸But Noah found favor with the LORD.

⁹"This is the history of Noah and his family. Noah was a righteous man, the only blameless man living on earth at the time. He consistently followed God's will and enjoyed a close relationship with him. ¹⁰Noah had three sons: Shem, Ham, and Japheth.

¹¹"Now the earth had become corrupt in God's sight, and it was filled with violence. ¹²God observed all this corruption in the world, and he saw violence and depravity everywhere. So God said to Noah, 'I have decided to destroy all living creatures, for the earth is filled with violence because of them. Yes, I will wipe them all from the face of the earth!'" (Genesis 6:5-13).

The judgment on man for not being able to live right according to his own conscience was the great Flood and the destruction of all life except for Noah's family.

"For forty days the floods prevailed, covering the ground and lifting the boat high above the earth. ¹⁸As the waters rose higher and higher above the ground, the boat floated safely on the surface. ¹⁹Finally, the water covered even the highest mountains on the earth, ²⁰standing more than twenty-two feet above the highest peaks. ²¹All the living things on earth died—birds, domestic animals, wild animals, all kinds of small animals, and all the people. ²²Everything died that breathed and lived on dry land. ²³Every living thing on the earth was wiped out—people, animals both large and small, and birds. They were all destroyed, and only Noah was left alive, along with those who were with him in the boat. [24]And the water covered the earth for 150 days" (Genesis 7:17-24).

3. Dispensation of Human Government.

After ten and a half months the water receded enough so that Noah and his family and the animals they took with them could leave the ark. Noah immediately made an altar and worshiped the Lord on the shore.

Man had failed to live according to God's rules by liberty or conscience. Now God instructed Noah to create a society based on the rule of government.

"God blessed Noah and his sons and told them, 'Multiply and fill the earth. [2]All the wild animals, large and small, and all the birds and fish will be afraid of you. I have placed them in your power. [3]I have given them to you for food, just as I have given you grain and vegetables. [4]But you must never eat animals that still have their lifeblood in them. [5]And murder is forbidden. Animals that kill people must die, and any person who murders must be killed. [6]Yes, you must execute anyone who murders another person, for to kill a person is to kill a living being made in God's image. [7]Now you must have many children and repopulate the earth. Yes, multiply and fill the earth!'" (Genesis 9:1-7).

The authority to take the life of a murderer is the ultimate authority of government. Mankind was again given authority over the world and told to go and populate it all. Now even the killing of animals for food was approved.

Did the rule of law prevent men from sinning against God? Man was told to scatter and fill the earth. One of Noah's descendants was Nimrod, described in Genesis 10:8 as a mighty hunter. He founded the cities of Babel and Nineveh, which came to be the capitals of the Babylonian and Assyrian empires.

"At one time the whole world spoke a single language and used the same words. [2]As the people migrated eastward, they found a plain in the land of Babylonia and settled there. ³They began to talk about construction projects. 'Come,' they said, 'let's make great piles of burnt brick and collect natural asphalt to use as mortar. ⁴Let's build a great city with a tower that reaches to the skies—a monument to our greatness! This will bring us together and keep us from scattering all over the world'" (Genesis 11:1-4).

In defiance to God the people built the Tower of Babel, rather than rely on Him. Instead of using government to help promote obedience to God, they used government to try to become like Him.

God's judgment came quickly. "'Come, let's go down and give them different languages. Then they won't be able to understand each other.' ⁸In that way, the LORD scattered them all over the earth; and that ended the building of the city. ⁹That is why the city was called Babel, because it was there that the LORD confused the people by giving them many languages, thus scattering them across the earth" (Genesis 11:7-9).

4. Dispensation of Promise.

After the failure of man to live according to liberty, conscience, or government, God chose a moon worshiper from the city of Ur in Mesopotamia. He told Abram to pack up and move to a land that God would give to him as the father of a new and great nation. Abram believed God.

"Then the LORD told Abram, 'Leave your country, your relatives, and your father's house, and go to the land that I will show you. ²I will cause you to become the father of a great nation. I will bless you and make you famous, and I will make you a blessing to others. ³I will bless those who bless you and curse those who curse you. All the families of the earth will be blessed through you.'

⁴"So Abram departed as the LORD had instructed him, and Lot went with him. Abram was seventy-five years old when he left Haran. ⁵He took his wife, Sarai, his nephew Lot,

and all his wealth—his livestock and all the people who had joined his household at Haran—and finally arrived in Canaan. ⁶Traveling through Canaan, they came to a place near Shechem and set up camp beside the oak at Moreh. At that time, the area was inhabited by Canaanites.

⁷"Then the LORD appeared to Abram and said, 'I am going to give this land to your offspring.' And Abram built an altar there to commemorate the LORD's visit" (Genesis 12:1-7).

It only took a few generations for Abraham's descendants to fail to live according to God's promise in the promised land.

"So Jacob left Beersheba, and his sons brought him to Egypt. They carried their little ones and wives in the wagons Pharaoh had provided for them. ⁶They brought their livestock, too, and all the belongings they had acquired in the land of Canaan. Jacob and his entire family arrived in Egypt" (Genesis 46:5-6).

After a generation in Egypt, God's judgment came on Israel, God's chosen people.

"So the Egyptians made the Israelites their slaves and put brutal slave drivers over them, hoping to wear them down under heavy burdens. They forced them to build the cities of Pithom and Rameses as supply centers for the king. ¹²But the more the Egyptians oppressed them, the more quickly the Israelites multiplied! The Egyptians soon became alarmed ¹³and decided to make their slavery more bitter still. ¹⁴They were ruthless with the Israelites, forcing them to make bricks and mortar and to work long hours in the fields" (Exodus 1:11-14).

5. Dispensation of Law.

After man's failure to live according to innocence, conscience, government, or promise, God allowed man to live under an itemized set of rules and regulations. God sen

them Moses to liberate them from bondage in Egypt and to give them the Mosaic Law, starting with the Ten Commandments.

"The Israelites arrived in the wilderness of Sinai exactly two months after they left Egypt. ²After breaking camp at Rephidim, they came to the base of Mount Sinai and set up camp there.

³"Then Moses climbed the mountain to appear before God. The LORD called out to him from the mountain and said, 'Give these instructions to the descendants of Jacob, the people of Israel: ⁴You have seen what I did to the Egyptians. You know how I brought you to myself and carried you on eagle's wings. ⁵Now if you will obey me and keep my covenant, you will be my own special treasure from among all the nations of the earth; for all the earth belongs to me. ⁶And you will be to me a kingdom of priests, my holy nation. Give this message to the Israelites.'

⁷"Moses returned from the mountain and called together the leaders of the people and told them what the LORD had said. ⁸They all responded together, 'We will certainly do everything the LORD asks of us.' So Moses brought the people's answer back to the LORD" (Exodus 19:1-8).

Most of the remainder of the Old Testament is the story of Israel's rebellion against God, His sending prophets to get them to repent, brief periods of obedience, and their repeated failures to "do everything the LORD " asked of them. They did not obey His commands or worship Him alone.

The Book of 2 Kings describes it this way. "But the Israelites would not listen. They were as stubborn as their ancestors and refused to believe in the LORD their God. ¹⁵They rejected his laws and the covenant he had made with their ancestors, and they despised all his warnings. They worshipped worthless idols and became worthless themselves. They followed the example of the nations around them, disobeying the LORD's command not to imitate them. ¹⁶They

defied all the commands of the LORD their God and made two calves from metal. They set up an Asherah pole and worshipped Baal and all the forces of heaven. [17]They even sacrificed their own sons and daughters in the fire. They consulted fortune-tellers and used sorcery and sold themselves to evil, arousing the LORD's anger" (2 Kings 17:14-17).

The ultimate rebellion against God by Israel was the rejection of God's Son, the Messiah, Jesus Christ. Matthew described Jesus' trial before the Roman governor Pontius Pilate when the leaders of Israel demanded Jesus' execution.

"Meanwhile, the leading priests and other leaders persuaded the crowds to ask for Barabbas to be released and for Jesus to be put to death. [21]So when the governor asked again, 'Which of these two do you want me to release to you?' the crowd shouted back their reply: 'Barabbas!'

[22]"'But if I release Barabbas,' Pilate asked them, 'what should I do with Jesus who is called the Messiah?' And they all shouted, 'Crucify him!'

[23]"'Why?' Pilate demanded. "What crime has he committed?' But the crowd only roared the louder, 'Crucify him!'

[24]"Pilate saw that he wasn't getting anywhere and that a riot was developing. So he sent for a bowl of water and washed his hands before the crowd, saying, 'I am innocent of the blood of this man. The responsibility is yours!'

[25]"And all the people yelled back, 'We will take responsibility for his death—we and our children!' (Matthew 27:20-25).

Israel failed to live under the Law. They ended up killing the very One who fulfilled the Law, their Savior. The judgment of God was not far away. Jesus Himself told what was to come.

"And when you see Jerusalem surrounded by armies, then you will know that the time of its destruction has arrived. [21]Then those in Judea must flee to the hills. Let those in

Jerusalem escape, and those outside the city should not enter it for shelter. ²²For those will be days of God's vengeance, and the prophetic words of the Scriptures will be fulfilled. ²³How terrible it will be for pregnant women and for mothers nursing their babies. For there will be great distress in the land and wrath upon this people. ²⁴They will be brutally killed by the sword or sent away as captives to all the nations of the world. And Jerusalem will be conquered and trampled down by the Gentiles until the age of the Gentiles comes to an end" (Luke 21:20-24).

In less than forty years, in A.D. 70, the Roman army destroyed Jerusalem, and the temple, and sent Jewish people fleeing across the world.

Man had failed again to live according to God's standards. Innocence, conscience, government, promise, and law had all proven to be no match for man's innate sinfulness.

6. Dispensation of Grace.

We live in the age of grace, or the Church Age. The previous chapters on the persons and work of the triune God, especially the work of Jesus Christ and the Holy Spirit for and in believers, typify this age.

When people, Jews or Gentiles, believe the good news about Jesus Christ they are saved and become part of His universal church. Our responsibility to God under grace is to believe in Jesus Christ, to put our faith in Him, to trust Him. To enjoy the benefits of the salvation we receive as a gift from God, we are to yield our wills to the will of God through God the Holy Spirit, who lives in us.

"God saved you by his special favor when you believed. And you can't take credit for this; it is a gift from God. ⁹Salvation is not a reward for the good things we have done, so none of us can boast about it. ¹⁰For we are God's masterpiece. He has created us anew in Christ Jesus, so that we can do the good things he planned for us long ago" (Ephesians 2:8-10).

God did create His plans a long time ago. The prophets Jeremiah and Ezekiel told of things to come hundreds of years before Christ.

While promises were made to Israel (See Jeremiah 31:31-33 and Ezekiel 36:26-27, discussed in the previous chapter on the Holy Spirit, page 87), it was revealed to the Apostle Paul that the church would being participating in the blessings of the New Covenant prior to the full realization to the nation of Israel.

One of the distinctives of dispensational theology is a real difference between Israel and the church. Others have thought that the church replaced Israel as God's chosen people. But there are many promises to Israel that have yet to be fulfilled. As mentioned earlier, if you take the Bible to mean what it says in plain language, consistently, it will lead you to be a dispensationalist. There is still a time coming when the promises to Israel will be fulfilled.

In spite of the grace of God in offering salvation, only a part of mankind accepts his free gift. Most refuse to believe the revelation given to them. Jesus said, "You search the Scriptures because you believe they give you eternal life. The Scriptures point to me! [40]Yet you refuse to come to me so that I can give you this eternal life" (John 5:39-40).

Paul added, "You should also know this, Timothy, that in the last days there will be very difficult times. [2]For people will love only themselves and their money. They will be boastful and proud, scoffing at God, disobedient to their parents, and ungrateful. They will consider nothing sacred. [3]They will be unloving and unforgiving; they will slander others and have no self-control; they will be cruel and have no interest in what is good. [4]They will betray their friends, be reckless, be puffed up with pride, and love pleasure rather than God. [5]They will act as if they are religious, but they will reject the power that could make them godly. You must stay away from people like that" (2 Timothy 3:1-5).

God's judgment on the unbelieving world is certain. "For that will be a time of greater horror than anything the world has ever seen or will ever see again. [22]In fact, unless that time of calamity is shortened, the entire human race will be destroyed. But it will be shortened for the sake of God's chosen ones" (Matthew 24:21-22).

"Then the kings of the earth, the rulers, the generals, the wealthy people, the people with great power, and every slave and every free person—all hid themselves in the caves and among the rocks of the mountains. [16]And they cried to the mountains and the rocks, "Fall on us and hide us from the face of the one who sits on the throne and from the wrath of the Lamb. [17]For the great day of their wrath has come, and who will be able to survive?"' (Revelation 6:15-17).

How many ways can God demonstrate to man that He is holy and we are not? Through the ages God provided every opportunity for man to live in a right relationship with Him and every time we failed. Innocence, conscience, government, promise, law, and simply grace—trusting God who offers everything freely to us—and every time man failed.

7. Dispensation of the Kingdom.

The Messiah, Jesus Christ, will rule the world for one thousand years from David's throne in the city of Jerusalem. "Blessed and holy are those who share in the first resurrection. For them the second death holds no power, but they will be priests of God and of Christ and will reign with him a thousand years" (Revelation 20:6).

The requirement for living in the kingdom dispensation will be submission to Christ, the perfect King. He will rule with grace and perfect justice. "And the Lord will be king over all the earth. On that day there will be one Lord—his name alone will be worshiped" (Zechariah 14:9).

Mankind, having failed to please God and live righteously under the other dispensations, will still not be able to submit to the perfect King. Only raptured and resurrected saints, and believers who survive the Tribulation, will enter the millennial kingdom at the start. These believers will have children over the next one thousand years, and many of these will refuse to submit to the reign of Christ. At the end of the one thousand years many will rebel against him and follow Satan, proving conclusively that without the grace of God we would all be doomed by our sin.

"When the thousand years end, Satan will be let out of his prison. [8]He will go out to deceive the nations from every corner of the earth, which are called Gog and Magog. He will gather them together for battle—a mighty host, as numberless as sand along the shore. [9]And I saw them as they went up on the broad plain of the earth and surrounded God's people and the beloved city. But fire from heaven came down on the attacking armies and consumed them.

[10]"Then the Devil, who betrayed them, was thrown into the lake of fire that burns with sulfur, joining the beast and the false prophet. There they will be tormented day and night forever and ever" (Revelation 20:7-10).

Final Judgment

[11]And I saw a great white throne, and I saw the one who was sitting on it. The earth and sky fled from his presence, but they found no place to hide. [12]I saw the dead, both great and small, standing before God's throne. And the books were opened, including the Book of Life. And the dead were judged according to the things written in the books, according to what they had done. [13]The sea gave up the dead in it, and death and the grave gave up the dead in them. They were all judged according to their deeds. [14]And death and the grave were thrown into the lake of fire. This is the second death—the lake of fire. [15]And anyone whose name was not found recorded in the Book of Life was thrown into the lake of fire" (Revelation 20:11-15).

"In the dispensations God has demonstrated every possible means of dealing with man. In every dispensation man fails and only God's grace is sufficient."[2]

The Eight Biblical Covenants

The biblical covenants provide distinctions within the various stages in human history revealed in the dispensations.

Two are conditional (Edenic and Mosaic) and required man to meet his obligations before God fulfilled His part of the covenant. Six are unconditional, in which the promises of God are guaranteed to be fulfilled in God's time and way.

1. The Edenic Covenant

Made in the Garden of Eden. Life and blessing or death and cursing, dependent on Adam's faithfulness. (Genesis 1:26-31; 2:16-17)

2. The Adamic Covenant

Made after the Fall. God's declaration of what life will be because of sin. (Genesis 3:16-19)

3. The Noahic Covenant

Made after the flood. Introduces human government as a means to curb sin. (Genesis 9:1-18)

4. The Abrahamic Covenant

After the Tower of Babel. The unconditional promise of personal blessing to Abraham, creation of the nation of Israel, and blessing (redemption) through Israel for the entire world. (Genesis 12:1-4; 13:14-17; 15:1-7; 17:1-8)

2   Ibid, p. 136.

5. **The Mosaic Covenant**

   Made through Moses to Israel while Israel was journeying from Egypt to the Promised Land. Blessings dependent on Israel's faithfulness. (Exodus 20:1-31:18)

6. **The Palestinian Covenant**

   Unconditional promise of Israel's final possession of the land. (Deuteronomy 30:1-10)

7. **The Davidic Covenant**

   God's unconditional promise of David's unending lineage, throne, and kingdom. (2 Samuel 7:4-16; 1 Chronicles 17:3-15)

8. **The New Covenant**

   Guaranteed salvation for the church and the future of Israel. The church enjoys the spiritual benefits of the New Covenant promised to Israel. (Jeremiah 31:31-33; Ezekiel 36:27; Ephesians 3:9-10)

Practical Life Application

You now have a significant key to unlocking the true story of world history from God's perspective. You can see God's hand through the biblical accounts. What do you think you should do about it? May I suggest reading the Bible with a new understanding? Read it on a regular basis with a systematic time and plan of study.

You know how the story ends. Christ will win. We will win. So we should live like it.

Are you under the Old Testament law, including the Ten Commandments? Are we to use the Ten Commandments? If so, how? See the next chapter for discussion of these questions.

Under the Law, giving to God's ministries was tithing. What are we to do about tithing? God has given us everything. We are stewards. Instead of a tithe, or ten percent, given as a requirement, we can give even more generously out of gratitude to God.

Since we live under the Dispensation of Grace what kind of attitude should we have toward God? You are free from guilt. As a Christian you are accepted, forgiven, and loved by God. Be grateful. Do the will of God from a grateful heart.

How would this attitude affect your relationship with other people? People seldom treat other people better than they believe God treats them. Offer grace to others.

Is there someone you need to forgive, or someone from whom you need ask forgiveness? Who? When are you going to do something about it?

Looking at man's role in the world, we realize that no matter how hard we try to be good, we can't. Understanding our own inabilities should humble us and give us a sincere attitude of thanksgiving and gratitude toward God. In spite of ourselves, Jesus loves us.

Chapter 9

Law and Grace

One of the great challenges of those who teach Biblical Christianity is to distinguish clearly between law and grace as the operating system we live under as believers. Understanding the different dispensations helps immensely. The Christian is not under the Law but is covered by grace. This makes all the difference in the world.

Christians Are *Not* under the Law

"Sin is no longer your master, for *you are no longer subject to the law*, which enslaves you to sin. Instead, *you are free by God's grace*" (Romans 6:14).

"So this is the point: *The law no longer holds you in its power*, because you died to its power when you died with Christ on the cross. And now you are united with the one who was raised from the dead. As a result, you can produce good fruit, that is, good deeds for God. ⁵When we were controlled by our old nature, sinful desires were at work within us, and the law aroused these evil desires that produced sinful deeds, resulting in death. ⁶But now we have been released from the law, for we died with Christ, and we are no longer captive to its power. *Now we can really serve God, not in the old way by obeying the letter of the law, but in the new way, by the Spirit*" (Romans 7:4-6).

"Well then, why was the law given? It was given to show people how guilty they are. But this system of law was to last only until the coming of the child to whom God's promise was made" (Galatians 3:19).

"Until faith in Christ was shown to us as the way of becoming right with God, we were guarded by the law. We were kept in protective custody, so to speak, until we could put our faith in the coming Savior. [24]Let me put it another way. *The law was our guardian and teacher to lead us until Christ came.* So now, through faith in Christ, we are made right with God. [25]But now that faith in Christ has come, we no longer need the law as our guardian. [26]So you are all children of God through faith in Christ Jesus" (Galatians 3:23-26).

What Is the Law?

The Mosaic Law can also be called the Mosaic Covenant. It was made between God and the nation of Israel at Mount Sinai a year after the Israelites left Egypt.

Here are some of the major passages about the Law.

Exodus 20-31 (The Ten Commandments, altars, slaves, personal injury, property, social responsibility, justice, festivals, construction plans, priests, the Sabbath)

Exodus 34-40 (A new copy)

Leviticus 1-27 (Offerings, priests, ceremonial clean and unclean animals, purification, diseases, sexual cleanliness, the Day of Atonement, blood, forbidden sex, holiness, festivals, Sabbath Year, Year of Jublilee, redemption of property, the poor and slaves)

Numbers 5:1-10:10 (purity, marital faithfulness, Nazirites, offerings, dedication of Levites, the fiery cloud, silver tassels)

Numbers 15 (offerings, penalties, tassels)

Numbers 18-19 (duties of Levites and priests, water purification)

Numbers 28-30 (offerings and vows)

Numbers 34-35 (boundaries of the land, towns for Levites)

Deuteronomy 1:1-31:13 (second giving of the Law)

We should especially take note of the following key passages.

Israel's responsibility:

Exodus 19:3-8 (keep all of the Law)

Exodus 24:4-8 (All the people of Israel responded, "We will do everything!")

Deuteronomy 28 (obey and be blessed, or disobey and be cursed. A conditional covenant.)

Israel's failure:

2 Kings 17:7-20 (they broke the Law in every way; false gods, child sacrifice)

Matthew 27:1-25 (Israel rejected the promised Messiah)

Israel's judgment:

Deuteronomy 28:63-66 (worldwide dispersion as punishment for disobedience)

Luke 21:5-24 (temple would be destroyed and persecution would come)

Purposes of the Law

God had several reasons for giving the Law.

"We were guarded by the law. We were kept in protective custody, so to speak, until we could put our faith in the coming Savior. [24]Let me put it another way. The law was our guardian and teacher to lead us until Christ came" (Galatians 3:23-24).

"Obviously, the law applies to those to whom it was given, for its purpose is to keep people from having excuses and to bring the entire world into judgment before God. [20]For no one can ever be made right in God's sight by doing what his law commands. For the more we know God's law, the clearer it becomes that we aren't obeying it" (Romans 3:19-20).

Looking at God's Law is like looking into a mirror with a dirty face. You know you're not clean, but the mirror can do nothing to remove the dirt.

"These are all the commands, laws, and regulations that the LORD your God told me to teach you so you may obey them in the land you are about to enter and occupy, [2]and so you and your children and grandchildren might fear the LORD your God as long as you live. If you obey all his laws and commands, you will enjoy a long life. [3]Listen closely, Israel, to everything I say. Be careful to obey. Then all will go well with you, and you will have many children in the land flowing with milk and honey, just as the LORD, the God of your ancestors, promised you. [4]Hear, O Israel! The LORD is our God, the LORD alone. [5]And you must love the LORD your God with all your heart, all your soul, and all your strength. [6]And you must commit yourselves wholeheartedly to these commands I am giving you today'" (Deuteronomy 6:1-4) .

The Law taught the Israelites about God and offered them a way of protection.

"When the LORD your God brings you into the land you are about to enter and occupy, he will clear away many nations ahead of you: the Hittites, Girgashites, Amorites, Canaanites, Perizzites, Hivites, and Jebusites. These seven nations are all more powerful than you. [2]When the LORD your God hands these nations over to you and you conquer them, you must completely destroy them. Make no treaties with them and show them no mercy. ³Do not intermarry with them, and don't let your daughters and sons marry their sons and daughters. ⁴They will lead your young people away from me to worship other gods. Then the anger of the LORD will burn against you, and he will destroy you. ⁵Instead, you must break down their pagan altars and shatter their sacred pillars. Cut down their Asherah poles and burn their idols. ⁶For you are a holy people, who belong to the LORD your God. Of all the people on earth, the LORD your God has chosen you to be his own special treasure" (Deuteronomy 7:1-6).

The Law was also designed to keep Israel distinct and preserved from the world around them as God's special, chosen people.

Many foods were forbidden to the Israelites. Every time they ate they had to make a decision to obey or not. Kosher or not? Compare this to the institution of the New Covenant by Jesus Christ when He took the bread and wine, the most common elements of dining in his day, and said every time we did this, we are to remember Him. Is our communion with Him only an occasional, religious ritual or observance, or do we demonstrate our real relationship with Him by acknowledging and remembering him every time we eat or drink? Under the Law people had to think about obedience to God every time they put something in their mouths. It was a requirement. Under grace, it is not a requirement but a privilege. Let this be application or "food for thought" for us.

"We know these laws are good when they are used as God intended. ⁹But they were not made for people who do what is right. They are for people who are disobedient and rebellious, who are ungodly and sinful, who consider nothing sacred and defile what is holy, who murder their father or mother or other people. ¹⁰These laws are for people who are sexually immoral, for homosexuals and slave traders, for liars and oath breakers, and for those who do anything else that contradicts the right teaching ¹¹that comes from the glorious Good News entrusted to me by our blessed God" (1 Timothy 1:8-11).

The Law restrained evil in Israel and promoted civil righteousness instead of anarchy.

What the Law Could Not Do

"The old system in the law of Moses was only a shadow of the things to come, not the reality of the good things Christ has done for us. The sacrifices under the old system were repeated again and again, year after year, but they were never able to provide perfect cleansing for those who came to worship. ²If they could have provided perfect cleansing, the sacrifices would have stopped, for the worshipers would have been purified once for all time, and their feelings of guilt would have disappeared. ³But just the opposite happened. Those yearly sacrifices reminded them of their sins year after year. ⁴For it is not possible for the blood of bulls and goats to take away sins" (Hebrews 10:1-4).

The Law could not make us perfect or accepted and forgiven by God.

"But only the high priest goes into the Most Holy Place, and only once a year, and always with blood, which he offers to God to cover his own sins and the sins the people have committed in ignorance. ⁸By these regulations the Holy Spirit revealed that the Most Holy Place was not open to the people as long as the first room and the entire system it represents were still in use" (Hebrews 9:7-8).

The Law could not give us access to God. In fact, laymen entering the Holy of Holies where God was, would die. Today under grace believers are indwelt by the Holy Spirit. Our bodies are temples of the Holy Spirit. We have immediate and permanent access to God Himself.

"Appoint Aaron and his sons to carry out the duties of the priesthood. Anyone else who comes too near the sanctuary must be executed!" (Numbers 3:10).

Duration of the Law

Jesus said, "Don't misunderstand why I have come. I did not come to abolish the law of Moses or the writings of the prophets. No, I came to fulfill them" (Matthew 5:17).

"For Christ has accomplished the whole purpose of the law. All who believe in him are made right with God" (Romans 10:4).

Christ came to fulfill the Law. He is the end of the Law.

Results of the Law

We have been looking at the Mosaic Law, but there are applicable principles for any manmade system of laws or works which involve our own efforts to become right with God.

Think about your own efforts to make yourself right with God. What were the results?

Law leads to guilt, fear, pride, lack of love, avoidance of God, judgmental attitudes toward others, a lack of joy, no peace or rest in your spiritual life, and rebellion growing out of hopelessness.

In the midst of our hopeless despair God's grace reaches out to us.

Understanding God's Timetable for Israel

In understanding the difference between law and grace, it's important to know God's timetable for the nation of Israel. One of the central passages was written by the Old Testament prophet Daniel about six hundred years before Christ.

"A period of seventy sets of seven has been decreed for your people and your holy city to put down rebellion, to bring an end to sin, to atone for guilt, to bring in everlasting righteousness, to confirm the prophetic vision, and to anoint the Most Holy Place. [25]Now listen and understand! Seven sets of seven plus sixty-two sets of seven will pass from the time the command is given to rebuild Jerusalem until the Anointed One comes. Jerusalem will be rebuilt with streets and strong defenses, despite the perilous times.

[26]"After this period of sixty-two sets of seven, the Anointed One will be killed, appearing to have accomplished nothing, and a ruler will arise whose armies will destroy the city and the Temple. The end will come with a flood, and war and its miseries are decreed from that time to the very end. [27]He will make a treaty with the people for a period of one set of seven, but after half this time, he will put an end to the sacrifices and offerings. Then as a climax to all his terrible deeds, he will set up a sacrilegious object that causes desecration, until the end that has been decreed is poured out on this defiler" (Daniel 9:24-27).

Each "set" refers to a period of seven years. Seventy sets (70 X 7 = 490 years) were decreed for Israel from the time of the command to rebuild Jerusalem. That decree was made on March 4, 444 B.C. This decree is also recorded in Nehemiah 2:1-8. Seven and sixty-two sets will pass until the Anointed One (the Christ) comes. Using the Hebrew 360-day year, it has been computed to be March 29, 33 A.D., the date of Jesus' triumphal entry into Jerusalem. Of course, we know He was rejected by the nation and crucified six days later. This effectively shut off Israel's time clock. The city was destroyed in A.D. 70. There is still a set to go on Israel's clock. This seven-year period is being held back by God for the eventual fulfillment of all the prophecies concerning the nation. In the New Testament we're told that the church and the age of grace were a mystery not revealed until the time of Christ.

Mark 7:24-30 records Jesus' only recorded miracle beyond the borders of the Promised Land.

"Then Jesus left Galilee and went north to the region of Tyre. He tried to keep it secret that he was there, but he couldn't. As usual, the news of his arrival spread fast. [25]Right away a woman came to him whose little girl was possessed by an evil spirit. She had heard about Jesus, and now she came and fell at his feet. [26]She begged him to release her child from the demon's control. Since she was a Gentile, born in Syrian Phoenicia, [27]Jesus told her, 'First I should help my own family, the Jews. It isn't right to take food from the children and throw it to the dogs.'

[28]"She replied, 'That's true, Lord, but even the dogs under the table are given some crumbs from the children's plates.'

[29]"'Good answer!' he said. 'And because you have answered so well, I have healed your daughter." [30]And when she arrived home, her little girl was lying quietly in bed, and the demon was gone."

Dr. Mark Bailey, president of Dallas Theological Seminary, has called this passage "the hinge of the Gospels." In it we see God turning His ministry away from Israel, which was beginning to reject Jesus, toward the Gentile world and making His blessings available to all. This would be part of the mystery of the church not previously revealed.

Matthew 27, records the ultimate rejection of Christ by the people of Israel. God then turned off Israel's clock for a time, now about two thousand years, but a day will come when that last seven years begins ticking down again.

The New Covenant of Grace

The New Covenant was promised by God back in the Old Testament, through the prophet Jeremiah, about six hundred years before Christ.

"The day will come,' says the LORD, 'when I will make a new covenant with the people of Israel and Judah. [32]This covenant will not be like the one I made with their ancestors when I took them by the hand and brought them out of the land of Egypt. They broke that covenant, though I loved them as a husband loves his wife,' says the LORD.

[33]"'But this is the new covenant I will make with the people of Israel on that day,' says the LORD. 'I will put my laws in their minds, and I will write them on their hearts. I will be their God, and they will be my people. [34]And they will not need to teach their neighbors, nor will they need to teach their family, saying, 'You should know the LORD.' For everyone, from the least to the greatest, will already know me,' says the LORD. 'And I will forgive their wickedness and will never again remember their sins'" (Jeremiah 31:31-34).

This covenant was made between God and the nation Israel. It has not yet been totally fulfilled, but the church partakes of the spiritual blessings of the covenant. The prophet Ezekiel, a contemporary of Jeremiah's, also talked about the New Covenant.

"For I will gather you up from all the nations and bring you home again to your land. [25]Then I will sprinkle clean water on you, and you will be clean. Your filth will be washed away, and you will no longer worship idols. [26]And I will give you a new heart with new and right desires, and I will put a new spirit in you. I will take out your stony heart of sin and give you a new, obedient heart. [27]And I will put my Spirit in you so you will obey my laws and do whatever I command. [28]And you will live in Israel, the land I gave your ancestors long ago. You will be my people, and I will be your God" (Ezekiel 36:24-28).

Let's look ahead to The New Testament for more information about the New Covenant. At the Last Supper, the night before He was to be crucified, Jesus talked about it. We celebrate this in the communion or the Lord's Table.

"After supper he took another cup of wine and said, "This wine is the token of God's new covenant to save you—an agreement sealed with the blood I will pour out for you" (Luke 22:20).

"And he took a cup of wine and gave thanks to God for it. He gave it to them and said, 'Each of you drink from it,

²⁸for this is my blood, which seals the covenant between God and his people. It is poured out to forgive the sins of many'" (Matthew 26:27-28).

In his Gospel, John added something to this same scene as he quoted Jesus.

"So now I am giving you a new commandment: Love eath other. Just as I have loved you, you should love each other. ³⁵Your love for one another will prove to the world that you are my disciples." (John 13:34-35)

The way we demonstrate our love for one another will witness to the world that we are Christ's disciples. How do we demonstrate love? Grace is God's love in action.

How you live your life demonstrating grace will glorify God. That's our command and our purpose.

One of the central passages in the New Testament on the New Covenant is Hebrews 8:1-13.

"Here is the main point: Our High Priest sat down in the place of highest honor in heaven, at God's right hand. ²There he ministers in the sacred tent, the true place of worship that was built by the Lord and not by human hands.

³"And since every high priest is required to offer gifts and sacrifices, our High Priest must make an offering, too. ⁴If he were here on earth, he would not even be a priest, since there already are priests who offer the gifts required by the law of Moses. ⁵They serve in a place of worship that is only a copy, a shadow of the real one in heaven. For when Moses was getting ready to build the Tabernacle, God gave him this warning: 'Be sure that you make everything according to the design I have shown you here on the mountain.' ⁶But our High Priest has been given a ministry that is far superior to the ministry of those who serve under the old laws, for he is the one who guarantees for us a better covenant with God, based on better promises.

[7]"If the first covenant had been faultless, there would have been no need for a second covenant to replace it. [8]But God himself found fault with the old one when he said: 'The day will come, says the Lord, when I will make a new covenant with the people of Israel and Judah. This covenant will not be like the one I made with their ancestors when I took them by the hand and led them out of the land of Egypt. They did not remain faithful to my covenant, so I turned my back on them, says the Lord.

[10]"'But this is the new covenant I will make with the people of Israel on that day, says the Lord: I will put my laws in their minds so they will understand them, and I will write them on their hearts so they will obey them. I will be their God, and they will be my people.[11]And they will not need to teach their neighbors, nor will they need to teach their family, saying, "You should know the Lord." For everyone, from the least to the greatest, will already know me.[12]And I will forgive their wrong doings, and I will never again remember their sins.'

[13]When God speaks of a new covenant, it means he has made the first one obsolete. It is now out of date and ready to be put aside" (Hebrews 8:1-13).

The author of Hebrews quoted from Jeremiah 31. One of the great joys of discovery in Bible study is to see how passages in the Old Testament and New Testament intertwine, building on and explaining one another. We can see God's sovereign plan unfold through all the ages.

For more on the Old and New Covenants read Hebrews 9-10.

Mystery of New Covenant Blessings for the Church

Paul's letter to the Ephesians talks about the reconciliation between Jews and Gentiles in Christ.

"Don't forget that you Gentiles used to be outsiders by birth. You were called 'the uncircumcised ones' by the Jews, who were proud of their circumcision, even though it affected only their bodies and not their hearts. [12]In those days you were living apart from Christ. You were excluded from God's people, Israel, and you did not know the promises God had made to them. You lived in this world without God and without hope. [13]But now you belong to Christ Jesus. Though you once were far away from God, now you have been brought near to him because of the blood of Christ.

[14]"For Christ himself has made peace between us Jews and you Gentiles by making us all one people. He has broken down the wall of hostility that used to separate us. [15]By his death he ended the whole system of Jewish law that excluded the Gentiles. His purpose was to make peace between Jews and Gentiles by creating in himself one new person from the two groups. [16]Together as one body, Christ reconciled both groups to God by means of his death, and our hostility toward each other was put to death. [17]He has brought this Good News of peace to you Gentiles who were far away from him, and to us Jews who were near. [18]Now all of us, both Jews and Gentiles, may come to the Father through the same Holy Spirit because of what Christ has done for us.

[19]"So now you Gentiles are no longer strangers and foreigners. You are citizens along with all of God's holy people. You are members of God's family. [20]We are his house, built on the foundation of the apostles and the prophets. And the cornerstone is Christ Jesus himself. [21]We who believe are carefully joined together, becoming a holy temple for the Lord. [22]Through him you Gentiles are also joined together as part of this dwelling where God lives by his Spirit.

"I, Paul, am a prisoner of Christ Jesus because of my preaching to you Gentiles. [2]As you already know, God has given me this special ministry of announcing his favor to you Gentiles. [3]As I briefly mentioned earlier in this letter, God himself revealed his secret plan to me. [4]As you read what I have written, you will understand what I know about this plan regarding Christ. [5]God did not reveal it to previous generations, but now he has revealed it by the Holy Spirit to his holy apostles and prophets.

[6]"And this is the secret plan: The Gentiles have an equal share with the Jews in all the riches inherited by God's children. Both groups have believed the Good News, and both are part of the same body and enjoy together the promise of blessings through Christ Jesus" (Ephesians 2:11-3:6).

Hebrews 10 also talks about the benefits to us under the New Covenant. We no longer need a sacrificial system, for we can go directly to the throne of God through Christ.

Law and Grace Do Not Mix

"When people work, their wages are not a gift. Workers earn what they receive. [5]But people are declared righteous because of their faith, not because of their work" (Romans 4:4-5).

"And if they are saved by God's kindness, then it is not by their good works. For in that case, God's wonderful kindness would not be what it really is—free and undeserved" (Romans 11:6).

Everyone wants to do something, anything, to prove they have some worth, and therefore deserve God's salvation. But the Bible clearly teaches that nothing we are or do in ourselves can help one bit. We are saved by simply accepting the free gift of God through trusting the finished work of Jesus Christ.

You can draw a line through history at the cross of Calvary. On one side is the Old Covenant and the Law. On the other side of the cross is the New Covenant and grace.

Let's illustrate and compare the two in the following illustration. [1]

The Cross

Law The Old Covenant	Grace The New Covenant
Works "Me" Self-centered	Faith "Christ" Other people centered
My will "Do this and live" Works of the flesh	God's will "Believe and live" Fruit of the Spirit (love, joy, peace, patience, kindness, goodness, faithfulness, gentleness, and self-control)
Condemns	Saves
Kills	Makes alive
Curses	Redeems from the curse
Exposes the distance between God and people	Reconciles people to God
Condemns the best person	Freely justifies the worst person
Sheep die for the shepherd	The Good Shepherd dies for His sheep

Under the Law people were motivated by wanting to receive external reward or avoid punishment. Under grace our motivation is an internal desire to please God.

1.   Tim Stevenson, TEAM Training Notes (Lewisville, Texas: Crossroads Bible Church, 1995).

Under Law access to God was limited to the high priest once a year. Under grace the Holy Spirit lives in us, and we have immediate, eternal access to God. He is always with us.

Forgiveness was conditional and incomplete. Today our forgiveness and acceptance are unconditional and complete. "It is finished!" (John 19:30).

Practical Life Application

You live in the Age of Grace. So don't put yourself under the Law. Live according to grace.

Be Christ-centered and other-person-centered instead of self-centered.

Yield your will to God's will. Do what He wants and not necessarily what you want. As you yield to the leading of the Holy Spirit you will enjoy the "fruit of the Spirit" in your life: love, joy, peace, patience, kindness, goodness, faithfulness, gentleness, and self-control.

If you are not experiencing one or more of the fruits in your life, it may be reflective of an area of your life where you are not yielding to the Holy Spirit. Examine yourself. Pray to be made willing to obey God.

We are reconciled to God forever. We have new life in Christ. The indwelling Holy Spirit makes us alive. Live your new life in a way that reflects well on God.

God has given us everything we need. We are free to love Him with all our hearts and to live in thankfulness and gratitude to Him.

Chapter 10

The Church

A few years ago a number of American flags were displayed in one of the older churches in town in honor of those families who had lost a loved one during military service. A young boy asked what the flags were for and one of the church's older saints explained that the flags were for those who had died in the service. The boy asked, "In the 9:00 or 10:30 service?"

Early twentieth century evangelist Billy Sunday said, "Going to church doesn't make you a Christian any more than going to a garage makes you an automobile."

What does the Bible really say about the church?

In the New Testament, the Greek word for "church" is *ekklesia*, from which we get words such as "ecclesiastic" and "clergy." It basically means a gathering of people. More specifically, it came to represent a group of "called out ones"—a unique, special group called out from everyone at large.

The Universal Church

Just before His ascension Jesus told his disciples something new was about to happen. "In one of these meetings as he was eating a meal with them, he told them, 'Do not leave Jerusalem until the Father sends you what he promised.

Remember, I have told you about this before. ⁵John baptized with water, but in just a few days you will be baptized with the Holy Spirit.'

⁶"When the apostles were with Jesus, they kept asking him, 'Lord, are you going to free Israel now and restore our kingdom?'

⁷"'The Father sets those dates,' he replied, 'and they are not for you to know. ⁸But when the Holy Spirit has come upon you, you will receive power and will tell people about me everywhere—in Jerusalem, throughout Judea, in Samaria, and to the ends of the earth'" (Acts 1:4-8).

We see the fulfillment of this prediction in Acts 2.

"On the day of Pentecost, seven weeks after Jesus' resurrection, the believers were meeting together in one place. ²Suddenly, there was a sound from heaven like the roaring of a mighty windstorm in the skies above them, and it filled the house where they were meeting. ³Then, what looked like flames or tongues of fire appeared and settled on each of them. ⁴And everyone present was filled with the Holy Spirit and began speaking in other languages, as the Holy Spirit gave them this ability" (Acts 2:1-4).

This was the start of the church. The New Testament talks about two things when it refers to the church. There are local groups of people in different cities. We'll look at the local church later. There is also the universal church, which began on the Day of Pentecost, and consists of all believers, Jews and Gentiles, formed by the baptism of the Holy Spirit, made one in Christ, and which will continue on earth until the rapture.

"The human body has many parts, but the many parts make up only one body. So it is with the body of Christ. ¹³Some of us are Jews, some are Gentiles, some are slaves, and some are free. But we have all been baptized into Christ's body by one Spirit, and we have all received the same Spirit" (1 Corinthians 12:12-13).

Note two things about this passage. First, "all" have been baptized into the church (Christ's body) by the Holy Spirit. Some people wrongly teach that this is an experience that occurs sometime *after* salvation. However, if "all" in the church are baptized by the Spirit, then the baptism of the Spirit must occur at the moment of conversion. The baptism referred to here is real. It is the baptism which comes with salvation. And there is not a drop of water in it.

"And God has put all things under the authority of Christ, and he gave him this authority for the benefit of the church. [23]And the church is his body; it is filled by Christ, who fills everything everywhere with his presence" (Ephesians 1:22-23).

"Christ is the head of the church, which is his body" (Colossians 1:18).

Believers in the church were first called "Christians" (followers of Christ) in the city of Antioch, as noted in Acts 11:26.

The Mystery of the Church

As noted earlier, the church was a mystery not revealed until the time of Christ. One of the keys to understanding the church is to recognize the differences between Israel and the church. Israel is not the church. The church did not replace Israel.

Paul distinguished between Jews, unbelieving Gentiles, and the church, "Don't give offense to Jews or Gentiles or the church of God" (1 Corinthians 10:32). This shows that the Jews and the church are distinct.

There are still unfulfilled promises God has made to the nation of Israel that will be literally fulfilled in the future.

God promised to make a new covenant with Israel. While that has not totally taken place with Israel yet (with spiritual and physical blessings for the nation), the church is benefiting, as already noted, from the spiritual blessing of the covenant. That is part of the mystery or secret explained by the apostle Paul.

"Just think! Though I did nothing to deserve it, and though I am the least deserving Christian there is, I was chosen for this special joy of telling the Gentiles about the endless treasures available to them in Christ. ⁹I was chosen to explain to everyone this plan that God, the Creator of all things, had kept secret from the beginning.

¹⁰"God's purpose was to show his wisdom in all its rich variety to all the rulers and authorities in the heavenly realms. They will see this when Jews and Gentiles are joined together in his church. ¹¹This was his plan from all eternity, and it has now been carried out through Christ Jesus our Lord" (Ephesians 3:8-11).

"God has given me the responsibility of serving his church by proclaiming his message in all its fullness to you Gentiles. ²⁶This message was kept secret for centuries and generations past, but now it has been revealed to his own holy people. ²⁷For it has pleased God to tell his people that the riches and glory of Christ are for you Gentiles, too. For this is the secret: Christ lives in you, and this is your assurance that you will share in his glory" (Colossians 1:25-27).

The church is also called the bride of Christ (Ephesians 5:32). The marriage and wedding feast between Christ and the church will take place in heaven (Revelation 19:7-9).

Prior to the wedding feast, the church will be raptured, or caught up into the air, by Christ.

"But let me tell you a wonderful secret God has revealed to us. Not all of us will die, but we will all be transformed. ⁵²It will happen in a moment, in the blinking of an eye, when the last trumpet is blown. For when the trumpet sounds, the Christians who have died will be raised with transformed bodies. And then we who are living will be transformed so that we will never die. ⁵³For our perishable earthly bodies must be transformed into heavenly bodies that will never die" (1 Corinthians 15:51-53).

"For the Lord himself will come down from heaven with a commanding shout, with the call of the archangel, and with the trumpet call of God. First, all the Christians who have died will rise from their graves. [17]Then, together with them, we who are still alive and remain on the earth will be caught up in the clouds to meet the Lord in the air and remain with him forever" (1 Thessalonians 4:16-17).

Foundation of the Church

The first use in the New Testament of the word for church, *ekklesia*, is found in Matthew when Jesus was talking to the apostles.

"When Jesus came to the region of Caesarea Philippi, he asked his disciples, 'Who do people say that the Son of Man is?' [14]'Well,' they replied, 'some say John the Baptist, some say Elijah, and others say Jeremiah or one of the other prophets.'

[15]"Then he asked them, 'Who do you say I am?' [16]Simon Peter answered, 'You are the Messiah, the Son of the living God.' [17]Jesus replied, 'You are blessed, Simon son of John, because my Father in heaven has revealed this to you. You did not learn this from any human being. [18]Now I say to you that you are Peter, and upon this rock I will build my church, and all the powers of hell will not conquer it. [19]And I will give you the keys of the Kingdom of Heaven. Whatever you lock on earth will be locked in heaven, and whatever you open on earth will be opened in heaven" (Matthew 16:13-19).

This passage has led to tremendous difficulties in understanding what the church really is. Part of that difficulty lies in translation. Let's try to illustrate this in English.

Is there a difference in the English words "log" and "lag"? There is only one small difference, just one letter. Yet that difference changes the meaning completely.

Many have used the passage in Matthew to say that Jesus built the church on Peter because He changed his name to "Rock" or "Peter." The Greek word for rock, which means a boulder or massive rock used as a foundation, is the Greek word *petras*. But that is not what the best manuscripts say Jesus called Peter. Jesus used the word "petros." Again, it's only one letter different, but it means something else. It comes closer to our nickname "Rocky." It is as if Jesus was using play on words. God had revealed to "Rocky" the truth that Jesus is the Messiah, the Son of God, and the church would be built on this foundation, not Peter.

Peter never claimed to be the foundation of the church. In fact, he said Christ was the foundation and he quoted from the Old Testament to prove it.

"Come to Christ, who is the living cornerstone of God's temple. He was rejected by the people, but he is precious to God who chose him. [5]And now God is building you, as living stones, into his spiritual temple. What's more, you are God's holy priests, who offer the spiritual sacrifices that please him because of Jesus Christ. [6]As the Scriptures express it, 'I am placing a stone in Jerusalem, a chosen cornerstone, and anyone who believes in him will never be disappointed.'

[7]"Yes, he is very precious to you who believe. But for those who reject him, "The stone that was rejected by the builders has now become the cornerstone" (1 Peter 2:4-7).

In verse 6 Peter was quoting from Isaiah 28:16, written 700 years earlier about the coming Messiah. In verse 7, Peter was obviously referring to the rejection of Christ and His death on the cross.

Also, Paul called Jesus the foundation. "For no one can lay any other foundation than the one we already have—Jesus Christ" (1 Corinthians 3:11).

For over a thousand years, from A.D. 100 on, the universal church and the local church were not differentiated. If you were in a local church, you were automatically assumed to be in the universal church. The physical church made rules defining what was required to be a part of the universal or spiritual church. The word for universal was "catholic." All Christians were in the catholic or universal church.

For the first several hundred years the church had two ordinances, which some call sacraments. These were water baptism and communion. As late as the fifth century, Augustine, the great bishop in the city of Hippo, said they were memorials to Christ and not means of salvation. During the Middle Ages, as the catholic church evolved into what became known as the Roman Catholic Church, five other ordinances were added (penance or confession, confirmation, marriage, holy orders, and last rites) and all seven were called sacraments. The Roman Catholic Church taught that those sacraments convey grace to those who participate in them. (After A.D. 600 the Eastern Orthodox churches formally announced their separation from Rome. They had never acknowledged Rome's authority over them.)

The Reformation and the Modern Period

The Reformers, led by former Roman Catholic scholars such as Martin Luther and John Calvin, redefined the universal church. Today, once again, the church is identified as the body of Christ, made up of all believers, people who have placed their faith in Jesus Christ and trust Him for their salvation.

As the church's definition changed, so did the rules of governance. How do you run a local church? Who leads it?

The Local Church

The local church today must be redefined from what it has been through most of history. It is obviously an assembly of people. Members of the local church should be members of the universal church, believers, although many who attend may not be believers. Ideally the church is always reaching out and attracting nonbelievers so it will never be filled one hundred percent with believers if it is functioning properly. This group will have some ordinances such as water baptism and communion. Many Brethren churches add foot washing as an ordinance. The group will have some sort of governing regulations or by-laws.

The following are several ways local churches are organized today.

Papal. The Roman Catholic Church is directed from the office of the pope with the assistance of the church hierarchy, cardinals, bishops, priests, and others.

Episcopal. The Church of England, Methodist, and Episcopal churches are governed by a hierarchy of leaders (bishops and others) who have authority over local churches.

Presbyterian. Elected and appointed representatives have authority over churches.

Congregational. Most Baptist, Church of Christ, and Congregational churches are democratically governed by members including the selection of deacons and pastors.

Elder rule. Most independent Bible churches are in this category. A group of elders who start a local church elect new or additional elders. These elders are responsible for the spiritual life of the local church. They hire pastors and appoint deacons for specific tasks such as maintaining the finances and facilities.

One-man rule. Often a strong founding pastor will run "his" church as he wants to, hopefully, with the advice and help of elders or deacons.

Each of these types of governing situations have strengths and weaknesses.

Leadership Qualifications

Several Bible passages discuss the qualifications for leadership in the church.

"It is a true saying that if someone wants to be an elder, he desires an honorable responsibility. [2]For an elder must be a man whose life cannot be spoken against. He must be faithful to his wife. He must exhibit self-control, live wisely, and have a good reputation. He must enjoy having guests in his home and must be able to teach. [3]He must not be a heavy drinker or be violent. He must be gentle, peace loving, and not one who loves money. [4]He must manage his own family well, with children who respect and obey him. [5]For if a man cannot manage his own household, how can he take care of God's church?

[6]"An elder must not be a new Christian, because he might be proud of being chosen so soon, and the Devil will use that pride to make him fall. [7]Also, people outside the church must speak well of him so that he will not fall into the Devil's trap and be disgraced.

[8]"In the same way, deacons must be people who are respected and have integrity. They must not be heavy drinkers and must not be greedy for money. [9]They must be committed to the revealed truths of the Christian faith and must live with a clear conscience. [10]Before they are appointed as deacons, they should be given other responsibilities in the church as a test of their character and ability. If they do well, then they may serve as deacons.

[11]"In the same way, their wives must be respected and must not speak evil of others. They must exercise self-control and be faithful in everything they do.

[12]"A deacon must be faithful to his wife, and he must manage his children and household well. [13]Those who do

well as deacons will be rewarded with respect from others and will have increased confidence in their faith in Christ Jesus" (1 Timothy 3:1-13).

"I left you [Titus] on the island of Crete so you could complete our work there and appoint elders in each town as I instructed you. ⁶An elder must be well thought of for his good life. He must be faithful to his wife, and his children must be believers who are not wild or rebellious. ⁷An elder must live a blameless life because he is God's minister. He must not be arrogant or quick-tempered; he must not be a heavy drinker, violent, or greedy for money. ⁸He must enjoy having guests in his home and must love all that is good. He must live wisely and be fair. He must live a devout and disciplined life. ⁹He must have a strong and steadfast belief in the trustworthy message he was taught; then he will be able to encourage others with right teaching and show those who oppose it where they are wrong" (Titus 1:5-9).

"And now, a word to you who are elders in the churches. I, too, am an elder and a witness to the sufferings of Christ. And I, too, will share his glory and his honor when he returns. As a fellow elder, this is my appeal to you: ²Care for the flock of God entrusted to you. Watch over it willingly, not grudgingly—not for what you will get out of it, but because you are eager to serve God. ³Don't lord it over the people assigned to your care, but lead them by your good example. ⁴And when the head Shepherd comes, your reward will be a never-ending share in his glory and honor.

⁵"You younger men, accept the authority of the elders. And all of you, serve each other in humility, for God sets himself against the proud, but he shows favor to the humble" (1 Peter 5:1-3).

"Our sister Phoebe, a deacon in the church in Cenchrea, will be coming to see you soon. ²Receive her in the Lord, as one who is worthy of high honor. Help her in every way you can, for she has helped many in their needs, including me" (Romans 16:1-2).

What the Local Church Is to Look Like

Nowhere does the Bible say exactly how a local church is to function. However, the New Testament does include some examples and principles.

"Those who believed what Peter said were baptized and added to the church—about three thousand in all. [42]They joined with the other believers and devoted themselves to the apostles' teaching and fellowship, sharing in the Lord's Supper and in prayer" (Acts 2:41-42).

Note several things about these believers. First, they were water baptized shortly after they trusted Christ. In some cultures it is still an immediate first step for new believers in their public identification with Christ and the church.

Second, they joined together. The Lord wants us to be in a local body of believers. It's part of His plan for our lives.

Third, they devoted themselves to the apostles' teaching. We call this Bible study and expository preaching, explaining what the prophets and apostles meant by what they said as recorded for us in the Bible.

Fourth, they were also devoted to fellowship. They got together often and enjoyed each other's company. Small groups that gather together several times every month follow this principle.

Fifth, they shared in the Lord's supper. This was a way of acknowledging the work of Jesus Christ for them. Other translations simply refer to this as the breaking of bread, that is eating together.

Sixth, they were devoted to prayer. Christians are to pray together. We can do this in a worship service on Sunday or a small group on a weeknight. Husbands and wives should pray together daily. Parents should pray with their children. Christians should be praying as a regular part of their daily lives. Praying keeps us in fellowship with God.

Ephesians 4:1-16 is one of the great New Testament passages about the local church.

"Therefore I, a prisoner for serving the Lord, beg you to lead a life worthy of your calling, for you have been called by God. ²Be humble and gentle. Be patient with each other, making allowance for each other's faults because of your love. ³Always keep yourselves united in the Holy Spirit, and bind yourselves together with peace.

⁴"We are all one body, we have the same Spirit, and we have all been called to the same glorious future. ⁵There is only one Lord, one faith, one baptism, ⁶and there is only one God and Father, who is over us all and in us all and living through us all. ⁷However, he has given each one of us a special gift according to the generosity of Christ. ⁸That is why the Scriptures say, 'When he ascended to the heights, he led a crowd of captives and gave gifts to his people.'

⁹"Notice that it says 'he ascended.' This means that Christ first came down to the lowly world in which we live. ¹⁰The same one who came down is the one who ascended higher than all the heavens, so that his rule might fill the entire universe.

¹¹"He is the one who gave these gifts to the church: the apostles, the prophets, the evangelists, and the pastors and teachers. ¹²Their responsibility is to equip God's people to do his work and build up the church, the body of Christ, ¹³until we come to such unity in our faith and knowledge of God's Son that we will be mature and full grown in the Lord, measuring up to the full stature of Christ.

¹⁴"Then we will no longer be like children, forever changing our minds about what we believe because someone has told us something different or because someone has cleverly lied to us and made the lie sound like the truth. ¹⁵Instead, we will hold to the truth in love, becoming more and more in every way like Christ, who is the head of his body, the church. ¹⁶Under his direction, the whole body is

fitted together perfectly. As each part does its own special work, it helps the other parts grow, so that the whole body is healthy and growing and full of love" (Ephesians 4:1-16).

We can divide this passage into three sections. The first section, verses 1-6, discusses the need for unity. There should be unity within the local church.

The second section, verses 7-12, discusses diversity. God has given us unique gifts to be used together for the good of the whole. In using our gifts in service to others, we are blessed. The third section, verses 13-16, deals with maturity. The church should be healthy and work together perfectly.

According to verse 12, who is to do the work in the church? Who are the ministers? God's people. Every one of us is in the ministry. In some churches only the professional staff are viewed as "ministers." The biblical job of the professional pastors and staff is "to equip God's people to do his work and build up the church." That is done by teaching the Bible, discipling, counseling, comforting, helping people understand their own giftedness, and providing encouragement and opportunities for people to use those gifts in service to others. A good local church will provide a path of growth for people to mature in their faith and service.

At Crossroads Bible Church, in Lewisville, Texas, Senior Pastor Tim Stevenson introduced a four-point philosophy to outline this growth path.

1. Every one a believer. The church will reach out to the community and provide opportunities for people to come to know and trust Christ. The main gathering device for this would be Sunday worship services.

2. Every believer a disciple. A disciple is a student. Wherever people are in the growth process, from kindergarden to mature adult, the church provides educational classes, groups, books, and other resources to help them learn more and grow.

3. Every disciple a servant. This vital part of the church's philosophy maintains balance for believers and helps keep them focused on others. The disciples are not "the few, the proud, the disciples." Every Christian should be growing and serving. The local church should promote opportunities for service.

4. Every servant a minister. When that service to God and others is part of the life motivation for a Christian, it is a ministry. Everyone in the church is a minister. The church should provide indepth leadership training to prepare people for a lifetime of ministry.

Spiritual Gifts

Many churches are like big sporting events in which a few participants in need of rest are watched by a large audience in need of exercise. This is not what the local church is intended to be. What's the problem?

The problem is threefold. The first is the lack of a defined mission statement, or philosophy of ministry, to accomplish the church's objectives to preach Christ and make disciples. The second is unused potential. God has given believers spiritual gifts to use in building up His church, but these gifts are often undiscovered, undeveloped, and unused. The third is wasted energy. Misdirected people are busy doing things they are not gifted to do. The solution is to understand and use our spiritual gifts.

Several passages in the Bible discuss spiritual gifts.

"Just as our bodies have many parts and each part has a special function, [5]so it is with Christ's body. We are all parts of his one body, and each of us has different work to do. And since we are all one body in Christ, we belong to each other, and each of us needs all the others.

[6]"God has given each of us the ability to do certain things well. So if God has given you the ability to prophesy, speak out when you have faith that God is speaking through you.

⁷"If your gift is that of serving others, serve them well. If you are a teacher, do a good job of teaching. ⁸If your gift is to encourage others, do it! If you have money, share it generously. If God has given you leadership ability, take the responsibility seriously. And if you have a gift for showing kindness to others, do it gladly" (Romans 12:4-8).

"He is the one who gave these gifts to the church: the apostles, the prophets, the evangelists, and the pastors and teachers. ¹²Their responsibility is to equip God's people to do his work and build up the church, the body of Christ, ¹³until we come to such unity in our faith and knowledge of God's Son that we will be mature and full grown in the Lord, measuring up to the full stature of Christ" (Ephesians 4:11-13).

"Most important of all, continue to show deep love for each other, for love covers a multitude of sins. ⁹Cheerfully share your home with those who need a meal or a place to stay.

¹⁰"God has given gifts to each of you from his great variety of spiritual gifts. Manage them well so that God's generosity can flow through you. ¹¹Are you called to be a speaker? Then speak as though God himself were speaking through you. Are you called to help others? Do it with all the strength and energy that God supplies. Then God will be given glory in everything through Jesus Christ. All glory and power belong to him forever and ever. Amen" (1 Peter 4:8-11).

"Now there are different kinds of spiritual gifts, but it is the same Holy Spirit who is the source of them all. ⁵There are different kinds of service in the church, but it is the same Lord we are serving. ⁶There are different ways God works in our lives, but it is the same God who does the work through all of us. ⁷A spiritual gift is given to each of us as a means of helping the entire church.

⁸"To one person the Spirit gives the ability to give wise advice; to another he gives the gift of special knowledge. ⁹The Spirit gives special faith to another, and to someone

else he gives the power to heal the sick. [10]He gives one person the power to perform miracles, and to another the ability to prophesy. He gives someone else the ability to know whether it is really the Spirit of God or another spirit that is speaking. Still another person is given the ability to speak in unknown languages, and another is given the ability to interpret what is being said. [11]It is the one and only Holy Spirit who distributes these gifts. He alone decides which gift each person should have" (1 Corinthians 12:4-11).

Paul then illustrated how differing gifts in the church are as necessary as different parts of the human body are essential for the overall functioning of the body. We need ears, eyes, a nose, feet, a heart, and so forth.

"Here is a list of some of the members that God has placed in the body of Christ: first are apostles, second are prophets, third are teachers, then those who do miracles, those who have the gift of healing, those who can help others, those who can get others to work together, those who speak in unknown languages.

[29]"Is everyone an apostle? Of course not. Is everyone a prophet? No. Are all teachers? Does everyone have the power to do miracles? [30]Does everyone have the gift of healing? Of course not. Does God give all of us the ability to speak in unknown languages? Can everyone interpret unknown languages? No! [31]And in any event, you should desire the most helpful gifts. First, however, let me tell you about something else that is better than any of them!"
(I Corinthians 12:28-31).

"Love will last forever, but prophecy and speaking in unknown languages and special knowledge will all disappear. [9]Now we know only a little, and even the gift of prophecy reveals little! [10]But when the end comes, these special gifts will all disappear.

[11]"It's like this: When I was a child, I spoke and thought and reasoned as a child does. But when I grew up, I put

away childish things. [12]Now we see things imperfectly as in a poor mirror, but then we will see everything with perfect clarity. All that I know now is partial and incomplete, but then I will know everything completely, just as God knows me now. [13]There are three things that will endure—faith, hope, and love—and the greatest of these is love" (1 Corinthians 13:8-13).

All of 1 Corinthians 12-14 deal with spiritual gifts and is worth reading.

Types of Spiritual Gifts

The New Testament discusses basic types of spiritual gifts. The first type were special "sign gifts" used by God to authenticate the message of the gospel and the messengers, Christ and the apostles, as they established the church and wrote the New Testament.

"So we must listen very carefully to the truth we have heard, or we may drift away from it. [2]The message God delivered through angels has always proved true, and the people were punished for every violation of the law and every act of disobedience. [3]What makes us think that we can escape if we are indifferent to this great salvation that was announced by the Lord Jesus himself? It was passed on to us by those who heard him speak, [4]and God verified the message by signs and wonders and various miracles and by giving gifts of the Holy Spirit whenever he chose to do so" (Hebrews 2:1-4).

Paul wrote, "When I was with you, I certainly gave you every proof that I am truly an apostle, sent to you by God himself. For I patiently did many signs and wonders and miracles among you" (2 Corinthians 12:12).

These sign gifts were to help start the church by building a foundation. By the end of the first century, the Bible had been completed and the church was well established in the Roman Empire.

These gifts, special abilities given to people, include apostleship, prophesy, discerning of spirits, word of wisdom, word of knowledge, miracles, healings, tongues or foreign languages, and the interpretation of foreign languages.

These gifts were temporary until the foundation could be established, as discussed in the 1 Corinthians 13. While God can certainly give any gifts He wants to at any time, it would seem that these sign gifts are no longer needed and are not the norm for today.

Miraculous gifts used to authenticate the messengers and their messages had happened before in the history of Israel. Moses could perform miracles. When they got to the Promised Land, the miracles died out. Elijah and Elisha performed miracles that also ended at the end of their lives. The third time miracles were seen in Israel as a sign was during and immediately after the time of Christ.

Spiritual Gifts for Today

Ephesians 4 says God gave these gifts to build up the church. Why? Verse 13 says, "until we come to such *unity* in our faith and knowledge of God's Son that we will be *mature and full grown in the Lord*."

Mature Christians will provide unity for the church as they serve one another with their spiritual gifts.

As we examine the various lists of spiritual gifts in Scripture, I believe we come to a total of ten or eleven. Let's examine each one.

1. **Evangelism**. This is evidenced by a passion for lost souls and the ability to present the gospel clearly. See Acts 21:8 for the example of Philip. Inherent dangers of this gift may be too much aggressiveness in witnessing or a desire to hear only evangelistic messages rather than sermons that teach and encourage.

2. **Pastoring/Shepherding**. Paul is our prime example of one with this spiritual gift. This involves the ability to teach and guide others toward a goal by providing spiritual leadership. It may also be accompanied by other gifts such as teaching, administration, or encouragement. A danger in this gift may be that the person may seem to be overbearing or to lack patience.

3. **Administration/Leadership**. This is the ability to make decisions and give directions for efficient operation and accomplishment of goals with harmony. Titus, as seen in Titus 1:5, is an example. The danger is to be too goal-oriented and to see people as resources while appearing to care more about the project than the people.

4. **Encouragement/Exhoration**. This is the ability to come alongside and help. It is the gift of drawing close to people in time of need to counsel and encourage. Barnabas (Acts 4:36; 9:27; 15:39) is an example of one with this gift. The danger is that one may become intolerant of systematic teaching and sound doctrine when not accompanied by practical application. The person may seem overconfident and results-oriented.

5. **Serving/Helping**. This is the gift of meeting the practical and material needs of others through the ability to perform any task or responsibility that helps and benefits others. Phoebe, a deaconess, is a good example (Romans 16:1). There can be a dangerous tendency to "do it yourself" rather than get other people involved in helping. Also a person with this gift may react negatively to those who are less sensitive to the needs of others.

6. **Mercy/Kindness**. This is the ability to show compassionate, practical, and cheerful love to those who are suffering. Barnabas is again an example. The danger is that persons with this gift may seem to lack firmness and to appear weak or indecisive.

7. **Giving**. This is the gift of cheerfully sharing material and financial resources with joy and without expectation of return. It is often accompanied by God's financial blessing. Dorcus is a good example (Acts 9:36). Sometimes there is a dangerous desire to try and control a ministry to make it more effective.

8. **Teaching**. This is the ability to explain the meaning of spiritual truth so that people understand and apply it. Priscilla and Aquila are examples (Acts 18:26). The danger with this gift is that the person may seem objective and logical but be lacking in warmth. Also he may be more interested in accuracy of facts, observation, and interpretation than in application.

9. **Faith**. This gift is the supernatural ability to have great confidence in God to do big things. It is an ability to believe deeply and boldly. This is the person who says, "Nothing is impossible because God is with us!" An example is Stephen (Acts 6:5). The danger is in appearing naïve or foolish by ignoring details or not counting the cost. This person may also put down others as unspiritual if they have different ideas.

10. **Hospitality**. This is the ability to welcome or befriend people quickly. People with this gift are great greeters and enjoy making people feel at home. They put people up in their homes and feed them. This gift could be part of the gift of encouragement or serving. The danger is that people with this gift may be taken advantage of or be hurt when others are not as open or hospitable.

11. **Prophecy**. The original gift of prophecy, proclaiming God's direct revelation, ceased with the completion of the New Testament. Today, some say the ability to discern motives, expose sin, and speak out quickly is a spiritual gift. These people usually love to memorize Scripture and are often impatient with the sins of others. The dangers here are obvious to the unity of the church.

What's Your Gift?

God has spiritually gifted each believer. How can you discern your spiritual gift or gifts?

What's the one thing you would like to do to really help build up and unify your church? Your answer may reveal the passion of your gift. We are all to exercise all the gifts in some way. We are all to give. We can all teach someone. We can all serve. We can all encourage. As we practice these things in the church, we will more likely discover the special ways God has gifted us beyond the average. Others will see it and can confirm it for us.

Pray about discovering your spiritual gifts. Review the biblical passages on spiritual gifts. Ask staff and friends in your church. Try exercising what you think is your gift or gifts. You'll enjoy it and you will be a blessing to others.

Practical Life Application

I have met Christians who said they didn't need to be in a local church. That is wrong. If you are a Christian, you are a member of the universal church. God's plan for His church is that we gather to worship and glorify Him and to demonstrate love for one another through service.

Believers should be in churches that teach the whole Word of God and help provide practical application of it to our lives.

How do you make sure you're in a good church or find one if you're not? Study the principlesab out church found in the Bible. Many of the them have been examined in this chapter. A good church will "preach Christ and make disciples," the motto of Crossroads Bible Church where I have had the privilege of serving as Pastor of Shepherding.

Seek to discover your spiritual giftedness and exercise those gifts in service to others. Ask someone in your church if they understand spiritual gifts and if they can help you discern what yours may be.

Chapter 11

Human Beings

Do you look like one of your parents? Is your personality similar? You may have heard the expression, "He's the spittin' image of his father," used to describe a son who looks exactly like his father. That phrase is actually a corruption of a principle taken from Genesis 1:26.

The New Living Translation says, "So God created people in his own image; God patterned them after himself; male and female he created them." Man was created in the spirit and image of God. "Spirit and image" became "spit' n' image" in spoken language and then became one of our English idioms.

How is man like God? Let's go back to the creation of man by God. Nature does not reveal how man is like God but Scripture does. First, man is not merely descended from animals. Man is a different kind of creature.

"So God created great sea creatures and every sort of fish and every **kind** of bird. And God saw that it was good. [22]Then God blessed them, saying, 'Let the fish multiply and fill the oceans. Let the birds increase and fill the earth.' [23]This all happened on the fifth day. [24]And God said, 'Let the earth bring forth every kind of animal—livestock, small animals, and wildlife.' And so it was. [25]God made all sorts of wild

animals, livestock, and small animals, each able to reproduce more of *its own kind*. And God saw that it was good.
Then God said, 'Let us make people in our image, to be like
ourselves. They will be masters over all life—the fish in the
sea, the birds in the sky, and all the livestock, wild animals,
and small animals.' So God created people in his own image;
God patterned them after himself; male and female he created them. [28]God blessed them and told them, 'Multiply and
fill the earth and subdue it. Be masters over the fish and
birds and all the animals'" (Genesis 1:21-28).

"And the LORD God formed a man's body from the dust
of the ground and breathed into it the breath of life. And the
man became a living person" (Genesis 2:7).

"And the LORD God said, 'It is not good for the man to be
alone. I will make a companion who will help him.' [19]So the
LORD God formed from the soil every kind of animal and
bird. He brought them to Adam to see what he would call
them, and Adam chose a name for each one. [20]He gave
names to all the livestock, birds, and wild animals. But still
there was no companion suitable for him. [21]So the LORD God
caused Adam to fall into a deep sleep. He took one of
Adam's ribs and closed up the place from which he had
taken it. [22]Then the LORD God made a woman from the rib
and brought her to Adam.

[23]"'At last!' Adam exclaimed. 'She is part of my own flesh
and bone! She will be called "woman," because she was
taken out of a man'" (Genesis 2:18-23).

Man and woman were created to be masters over all life.
Having the authority to name something means you have
authority over it. Man is not descended from animals. He is
a different kind of being, and he was given authority over
the world by God. Man is God's crowning work of creation.

The Nature of Man

Each person consists of two parts: material and immaterial. The material part is obvious. We have bodies. We are made of flesh and bones and blood. Since God is a spirit, we cannot be like God in our physical sense. In fact, God had to become like man physically through the incarnation of the Son in order to substitute for man and pay the penalty for sin in his place.

In our immaterial nature we are like God. We use many words to talk about the immaterial part of man: spirit, soul, heart, mind, will, emotions, conscience, and others. They involve our ability to think, create, and feel. The Bible often talks about our material and immaterial nature.

"Though our bodies are dying, our spirits are being renewed every day" (2 Corinthians 4:16).

"But this precious treasure—this light and power that now shine within us—is held in perishable containers, that is, in our weak bodies" (2 Corinthians 4:7).

"Don't be afraid of those who want to kill you. They can only kill your body; they cannot touch your soul" (Matthew 10:28).

"Yes, remember your Creator now while you are young, before the silver cord of life snaps and the golden bowl is broken. Don't wait until the water jar is smashed at the spring and the pulley is broken at the well. ⁷For then the dust will return to the earth, and the spirit will return to God who gave it" (Ecclesiastes 12:6-7).

The Fall of Man

When Adam and Eve were in the Garden of Eden things were very good. "Then God looked over all he had made, and he saw that it was excellent in every way. This all happened on the sixth day" (Genesis 1:31).

Then God gave them a test of obedience. "The LORD God placed the man in the Garden of Eden to tend and care for it. [16]But the LORD God gave him this warning: 'You may freely eat any fruit in the garden [17]except fruit from the tree of the knowledge of good and evil. If you eat of its fruit, you will surely die'" (Genesis 2:15-17).

In Genesis 3 we see how Adam and Eve sinned and what the consequences were.

"Now the serpent was the shrewdest of all the creatures the LORD God had made. 'Really?' he asked the woman. 'Did God really say you must not eat any of the fruit in the garden?'

[2]"'Of course we may eat it,' the woman told him. [3]'It's only the fruit from the tree at the center of the garden that we are not allowed to eat. God says we must not eat it or even touch it, or we will die.'

[4]"'You won't die!' the serpent hissed. [5]'God knows that your eyes will be opened when you eat it. You will become just like God, knowing everything, both good and evil.'

[6]"The woman was convinced. The fruit looked so fresh and delicious, and it would make her so wise! So she ate some of the fruit. She also gave some to her husband, who was with her. Then he ate it, too. [7]At that moment, their eyes were opened, and they suddenly felt shame at their naked-ness. So they strung fig leaves together around their hips to cover themselves.

[8]"Toward evening they heard the LORD God walking about in the garden, so they hid themselves among the trees. [9]The LORD God called to Adam, 'Where are you?'

[10]"He replied, 'I heard you, so I hid. I was afraid because I was naked.' [11]'Who told you that you were naked?' the LORD God asked. 'Have you eaten the fruit I commanded you not to eat?'

¹²"'Yes,' Adam admitted, 'but it was the woman you gave me who brought me the fruit, and I ate it.' ¹³Then the LORD God asked the woman, 'How could you do such a thing?' 'The serpent tricked me,' she replied. 'That's why I ate it.'

¹⁴"So the LORD God said to the serpent, 'Because you have done this, you will be punished. You are singled out from all the domestic and wild animals of the whole earth to be cursed. You will grovel in the dust as long as you live, crawling along on your belly. ¹⁵From now on, you and the woman will be enemies, and your offspring and her offspring will be enemies. He will crush your head, and you will strike his heel.'

¹⁶"Then he said to the woman, 'You will bear children with intense pain and suffering. And though your desire will be for your husband, he will be your master.'

¹⁷"And to Adam he said, 'Because you listened to your wife and ate the fruit I told you not to eat, I have placed a curse on the ground. All your life you will struggle to scratch a living from it. ¹⁸It will grow thorns and thistles for you, though you will eat of its grains. ¹⁹All your life you will sweat to produce food, until your dying day. Then you will return to the ground from which you came. For you were made from dust, and to the dust you will return.'

²⁰"Then Adam named his wife Eve, because she would be the mother of all people everywhere. ²¹And the LORD God made clothing from animal skins for Adam and his wife.

²²"Then the LORD God said, 'The people have become as we are, knowing everything, both good and evil. What if they eat the fruit of the tree of life? Then they will live forever!' ²³So the LORD God banished Adam and his wife from the Garden of Eden, and he sent Adam out to cultivate the ground from which he had been made. ²⁴After banishing them from the garden, the LORD God stationed mighty angelic beings to the

east of Eden. And a flaming sword flashed back and forth, guarding the way to the tree of life" (Genesis 3:1-24).

After they sinned, death entered the world. Mankind became subject to spiritual and physical death. They would "surely die." The serpent would crawl on the earth. Satan would one day be crushed by the offspring of a woman (Jesus). Women would experience extreme pain in childbirth and would live in conflict over authority with their husbands. The earth itself was cursed to be filled with thorns, and man would labor hard to produce food.

Though the judgment was severe, we should not think we would do better than Adam and Eve. We too are still tempted in the same ways and fail regularly.

"For the world offers only the lust for physical pleasure, the lust for everything we see, and pride in our possessions" (1 John 2:16). We want everything Adam and Eve wanted.

Let's look at the effect of Adam's sin on the human race.

First, Adam is our representative as the federal head of our race. Therefore we have imputed or judicial sin. Adam was our representative as the first man. He sinned. Therefore, we have to live with the consequences, just as we have to live with laws passed by our governmental representatives. Second, we are all physically descended from Adam, so we have an inherited sin nature, passed on from father to son. Third, we are all under the curse and the power of sin. Fourth, because we are all sinners by nature, we all personally sin.

In a nutshell, fallen mankind is depraved. The Bible talks about it in many passages.

"The human heart is most deceitful and desperately wicked" (Jeremiah 17:9).

"For all have sinned; all fall short of God's glorious standard" (Romans 3:23).

"Once you were dead, doomed forever because of your many sins. ²You used to live just like the rest of the world, full of sin, obeying Satan, the mighty prince of the power of the air. He is the spirit at work in the hearts of those who refuse to obey God. ³All of us used to live that way, following the passions and desires of our evil nature. We were born with an evil nature, and we were under God's anger just like everyone else.

⁴"But God is so rich in mercy, and he loved us so very much, ⁵that even while we were dead because of our sins, he gave us life when he raised Christ from the dead. (It is only by God's special favor that you have been saved!)" (Ephesians 2:1-5).

The great passage on the judgment of sin through Adam and Christ's contrasting victory over it is Romans 5:12-21.

"When Adam sinned, sin entered the entire human race. Adam's sin brought death, so death spread to everyone, for everyone sinned. ¹³Yes, people sinned even before the law was given. And though there was no law to break, since it had not yet been given, ¹⁴they all died anyway—even though they did not disobey an explicit commandment of God, as Adam did. What a contrast between Adam and Christ, who was yet to come! ¹⁵And what a difference between our sin and God's generous gift of forgiveness. For this one man, Adam, brought death to many through his sin. But this other man, Jesus Christ, brought forgiveness to many through God's bountiful gift. ¹⁶And the result of God's gracious gift is very different from the result of that one man's sin. For Adam's sin led to condemnation, but we have the free gift of being accepted by God, even though we are guilty of many sins. ¹⁷The sin of this one man, Adam, caused death to rule over us, but all who receive God's wonderful, gracious gift of righteousness will live in triumph over sin and death through this one man, Jesus Christ.

¹⁸"Yes, Adam's one sin brought condemnation upon everyone, but Christ's one act of righteousness makes all

people right in God's sight and gives them life. [19]Because one person disobeyed God, many people became sinners. But because one other person obeyed God, many people will be made right in God's sight.

[20]"God's law was given so that all people could see how sinful they were. But as people sinned more and more, God's wonderful kindness became more abundant. [21]So just as sin ruled over all people and brought them to death, now God's wonderful kindness rules instead, giving us right standing with God and resulting in eternal life through Jesus Christ our Lord" (Romans 5:12-21).

Christ provides us with judicial and actual satisfaction for sin.

What Is Sin?

In our modern world the word "sin" is almost obsolete. Human speculation has three alternative views. First, everything is relative. There is no right and wrong at all. We can all do whatever we want to do. A second view is that there is only a physical universe with no spiritual quality at all. There is no God. The third view is that sin is simply selfishness. Some selfish act may not be the best for mankind but the consequences are human.

Chafer and Walvoord define sin this way: "The teaching of Scripture is that sin is any want of conformity to the character of God, whether it be an act, disposition, or state."[1]

Four elements of sin were discussed concerning Adam. Let's review. First, there is imputed sin, the judicial standing we have because Adam is our representative. Second, we all have a sin nature passed on from our parents, all the way back to Adam. We are depraved. Third, we are all under the curse and power of sin. Fourth, there are personal sins we

---

1.   Chafer and Walvoord, *Major Bible Themes*, p. 178.

commit. This can be anything which misses the mark or standard of God's perfect holiness.

Salvation from the Penalty and Power of Sin

The prophet Jonah said, "For my salvation comes from the Lord alone" (Jonah 2:9).

We have all sinned. Romans 6:23 says we are all therefore deserving of death because "the wages of sin is death."

But we do not get what we deserve or have earned, namely, death, when we put our faith in Christ. He has solved our problem. He does more than restore us to Adam's innocence.

"All this newness of life is from God, who brought us back to himself through what Christ did. And God has given us the task of reconciling people to him. [19]For God was in Christ, reconciling the world to himself, no longer counting people's sins against them. This is the wonderful message he has given us to tell others. [20]We are Christ's ambassadors, and God is using us to speak to you. We urge you, as though Christ himself were here pleading with you, 'Be reconciled to God!' [21]For God made Christ, who never sinned, to be the offering for our sin, so that we could be made right with God through Christ" (2 Corinthians 5:18-21).

"But now God has shown us a different way of being right in his sight—not by obeying the law but by the way promised in the Scriptures long ago. [22]We are made right in God's sight when we trust in Jesus Christ to take away our sins. And we all can be saved in this same way, no matter who we are or what we have done.

[23]"For all have sinned; all fall short of God's glorious standard. [24]Yet now God in his gracious kindness declares us not guilty. He has done this through Christ Jesus, who has freed us by taking away our sins. [25]For God sent Jesus to take the punishment for our sins and to satisfy God's anger against us. We are made right with God when we believe

that Jesus shed his blood, sacrificing his life for us. God was being entirely fair and just when he did not punish those who sinned in former times. [26]And he is entirely fair and just in this present time when he declares sinners to be right in his sight because they believe in Jesus" (Romans 3:21-26).

"All honor to the God and Father of our Lord Jesus Christ, for it is by his boundless mercy that God has given us the privilege of being born again. Now we live with a wonderful expectation because Jesus Christ rose again from the dead" (1 Peter 1:3).

Practical Life Application

How should we respond to these biblical truths ?

Christ saved us from the penalty of sin and from the power of sin by giving us new life. I can do nothing to save myself. It is a gift of God. If you have not acted on this knowledge by trusting Christ and receiving Him through faith, then you should do it now and accept the Lord Jesus Christ as your savior.

As you understand your sinfulness and depravity, you should be humbled and grateful that Christ died for you. "But God showed his great love for us by sending Christ to die for us while we were still sinners" (Romans 5:8).

Because you have been forgiven much, you should be a forgiving person.

Even though we are now a fallen and tarnished image, human beings are still made in the spirit and image of God. We should be respectful of all human life. Regenerated Christians have stood against the evils of the Holocaust, genocide, abortion, and euthanasia.

As a saved and regenerated Christian with new life, what should be our response to Christ in light of the following verses?

"I have been crucified with Christ. [20]I myself no longer live, but Christ lives in me. So I live my life in this earthly body by trusting in the Son of God, who loved me and gave himself for me" (Galatians 2:19-20).

"Since you have been raised to new life with Christ, set your sights on the realities of heaven, where Christ sits at God's right hand in the place of honor and power. [2]Let heaven fill your thoughts. Do not think only about things down here on earth. [3]For you died when Christ died, and your real life is hidden with Christ in God. [4]And when Christ, who is your real life, is revealed to the whole world, you will share in all his glory" (Colossians 3:1-4).

You can overcome your old sin nature by allowing Christ to live His life through you. How can you do this? By surrendering your will to God's will. He loves you more than anyone else does. He loves you more than you love yourself, and He knows you perfectly. He knows everything. He Himself is perfect. His will for you must be perfect. You should make it a goal of life to know and follow His will for your life.

How can you know His will for your life? You need to read His Word, and study and meditate on it. You need to be in a church where His Word is taught from the pulpit and in classes and small groups. You need to be interactive in regular fellowship with other growing believers. You need to read good books on Christian living.

He is looking for your response. "The eyes of the LORD search the whole earth in order to strengthen those whose hearts are fully committed to him" (2 Chronicles 16:9).

As human beings, where do we turn to fulfill our deepest needs? Our Creator God made us and knows exactly what we need. He is also the source of all we need.

"As the deer pants for streams of water, so I long for you, O God. I thirst for God, the living God. When can I come and stand before him?" (Psalm 42: 1-2).

When Jesus was talking with the woman at the well, He said, "People soon become thirsty again after drinking this water. ¹⁴But the water I give them takes away thirst altogether. It becomes a perpetual spring within them, giving them eternal life" (John 4:13-14).

Human beings were designed to operate in a close relationship with God. Cars were designed to operate with gasoline. Without fuel, a car is still a car. You can sit in it. You can even push it around town. A pen was designed to write with ink. Without ink it is still a pen, but it is not very useful. Man without God is still a man, but he is not functioning the way God designed people to function.

We are born with a sin nature, separated from a holy God, and unable to function properly. Something deep in us, that tarnished image of God we carry, longs for restoration with our Creator. We desire His unconditional love. Most human beings flesh out this missing love of God in reference to significance and security. Men have a designed-in need to feel valued and important. Women especially have a strong need to feel safe and secure. From an early age we devise strategies to get these needs met, and strategies to avoid the empty feelings of not having these needs filled.

At the moment of salvation, when we trust Christ, the Holy Spirit comes to indwell us. We are given new spiritual life. For most people, however, instead of yielding to the power of the Holy Spirit in us, we yield to our old strategies to try and fill us up with the feelings we so powerfully desire. These strategies may have worked for a while and may have given us something of what we desired. That's why we use them. Since we established these strategies apart from God, they do not fully satisfy us. In fact, the longer we use them, the less satisfying they become. We may find ourselves on a vicious, downward cycle of addiction to whatever fuels our old strategies, only to be left more discouraged and depressed when they satisfy us for shorter and shorter periods. Any strategy we pursue to give us life, apart from God, becomes an idol. Idol worship, like all sin, falls short of the glory of God and does not ultimately satisfy. It doesn't really work. God will tolerate no false idols before Him. He alone wants to fill us and He does so as we yield to the Holy Spirit, instead of yielding to our old strategies.

"For my people have done two evil things: They have forsaken me—the fountain of living water. And they have dug for themselves cracked cisterns that can hold no water at all!" (Jeremiah 2:13).

What strategies have you used in your life to feel good and avoid feeling bad? Are they idols you go to instead of trusting Christ at a deeper level?

Sometimes we can simply obey as things are revealed to us. Other times we need to examine our deeply held strategies and see what happened to make us believe they were true. Remember, anything apart from God can only be partially true, at best. What worked for us to cope with life may be running out of gas and no longer working. They may be cracked cisterns. God may be calling you to change the way you think about these life strategies.

According to Romans 12:2, we are changed or transformed by renewing our minds. "Let God transform you into a new person by changing the way you think."

The truth is that only Christ can satisfy your deepest needs. Put aside your old ways by thinking them through, see their inadequacy, and deepen your trust in Christ. He alone will never leave you or forsake you and that is the greatest security you can have. He gave His life for you, proving once and for all how valuable you really are.

Chapter 12

Christian Living

How do I live the Christian life? How do I get from point A to point Z, from earth to heaven? How am I supposed to live? How can I live a godly life while living in such an ungodly world? All Christians ask these questions or ones much like them. This may be even more true for those who have been Christians for a little while.

When people put their trust in Christ, they are often excited about being in a local church, about discovering biblical truths, and about making changes in their lifestyle, all with the result of new blessings in life that help them develop confidence in their new-found faith.

This is sometimes followed by a time of testing or trial. Old habits or consequences of past behavior poke their ugly heads into the new life, and it starts to feel like the old life once again. Some even question their salvation.

Most of us want to deepen and enrich our spiritual lives. We'd like to experience a closer relationship with God. Don't you want to really feel God's love, to have a strong sense and knowledge of His presence in your life? That's what life is supposed to be for a Christian. That's His plan for us—life to the maximum!

Unfortunately many of us spend a lot of time hoping for these feelings and only catching glimpses of this victorious life here and there. Sometimes we feel we are drifting through life, hurting, not feeling very good about today and not very sure about tomorrow.

But God said, "'For I know the plans I have for you,' says the LORD. 'They are plans for good and not for disaster, to give you a future and a hope'" (Jeremiah 29:11).

That is good news. Be encouraged.

Christians are Holy, Set Apart, Saints

Believers are "holy," "set apart" for God. We are called "saints" throughout the New Testament. Each word has the same root in the Old and New Testament. We are to be in the world but different from the world, set apart "from" worldliness and set apart "for" God. The theological word for this is "sanctification."

Sanctification has three aspects. The first is positional sanctification. It is part of our justification. We are justified once and forever, based on Christ. "And what God wants is for us to be made holy by the sacrifice of the body of Jesus Christ once for all time" (Hebrews 10:10). When we trust Christ, we are positionally "made holy" or set apart for Him.

The second aspect is experiential sanctification. This involves the process of Christian growth and maturity.

The third aspect is ultimate sanctification or glorification when we are in heaven. "Now may the God of peace make you holy in every way, and may your whole spirit and soul and body be kept blameless until that day when our Lord Jesus Christ comes again. [24]God, who calls you, is faithful; he will do this" (1 Thessalonians 5:23-24).

"And we know that God causes everything to work together for the good of those who love God and are called according to his purpose for them. [29]For God knew his people in advance, and he chose them to become like his Son, so that his Son would be the firstborn, with many brothers and sisters. [30]And having chosen them, he called them to come to him. And he gave them right standing with himself, and he promised them his glory" (Romans 8:28-30).

In God's view we will certainly be glorified. He called us, knew us in advance, chose us, gave us a right standing before Him judicially (justified us), and has promised us His glory. It is a complete package. God does it all. We can be certain of our eventual glory with Him in heaven.

Why was man created? What are we set apart for? Major Ian Thomas describes it something like this. "We are set apart to fulfill the intelligent purposes for which we were intelligently made by an intelligent Creator."[1] Remember, we were created to glorify God. We are truly functional, as intended by our Creator, when others see in us the glory of God.

God is perfect, sinless, flawless. "Yet we were created to perfectly reflect the divine nature—a physical, visible, and audible expression of the invisible God."[2] Mankind failed when sin entered the world. Sin is a transgression of God's image. We fall short and tarnish God's image and reputation.

God's answer to the problem of sin was to send a perfect man, Jesus Christ. When we place our faith in Christ, we begin to grow in our knowledge and understanding of God. It is God's plan for Christ to live His life through us.

Practical Life Application

Most of this chapter deals with practical life application. Here are some suggestions on how can we live a holy life.

---

1.   Major Ian Thomas, lecture series (Lewisville, Texas: Crossroads Bible Church, 1999).
2.   Ibid.

A Change of Perspective and Attitude

First, our living a holy life starts with a change of perspective and attitude. It is not so much our living a holy life as it is Christ living His life through us. Let's look at some verses that will help us understand this concept.

"God has given us the privilege of being born again. Now we live with a wonderful expectation because Jesus Christ rose again from the dead" (1 Peter 1:3).

We are born again. We have new life through the resurrection of Jesus Christ.

"I have been crucified with Christ. [20]I myself no longer live, but Christ lives in me. So I live my life in this earthly body by trusting in the Son of God, who loved me and gave himself for me" (Galatians 2:19-20).

"Since you have been raised to new life with Christ, set your sights on the realities of heaven, where Christ sits at God's right hand in the place of honor and power. [2]Let heaven fill your thoughts. Do not think only about things down here on earth. [3]For you died when Christ died, and your real life is hidden with Christ in God. [4]And when Christ, who is your real life, is revealed to the whole world, you will share in all his glory.

[5]"So put to death the sinful, earthly things lurking within you. Have nothing to do with sexual sin, impurity, lust, and shameful desires. Don't be greedy for the good things of this life, for that is idolatry. [6]God's terrible anger will come upon those who do such things. [7]You used to do them when your life was still part of this world. [8]But now is the time to get rid of anger, rage, malicious behavior, slander, and dirty language. [9]Don't lie to each other, for you have stripped off your old evil nature and all its wicked deeds. [10]In its place you have clothed yourselves with a brand-new nature that is continually being renewed as you learn more and more about Christ, who created this new nature within you" (Colossians 3:1-10).

Live your life from God's perspective, as if Christ is living your life and you are seated in heaven. That is a wonderful perspective for overcoming temptation and old habits. Imagine you are looking down from heaven at Jesus living your life. "What would Jesus do?" is a good motto for living the Christian life, especially when facing temptation.

Be a Disciple

A second way of looking at how we can experience a holy life involves intentional choices we can make to follow Christ. A disciple is a learner, a student. Christ is the Good Shepherd, and we are members of His flock. As members of His flock we can live our lives in such a way that we witness for Him. Our lives can make Christ look good.

What are some of the marks of a disciple? In keeping with the shepherd-and-flock metaphor let's look at six marks of a disciple in the Gospel of John, using the acronym **FLOCKS.**

F—Faith. A member of the flock must have faith in Christ. "For God so loved the world that he gave his only Son, so that everyone who believes in him will not perish but have eternal life" (John 3:16).

L—Love. Members of Christ's flock will love one another. "I command you to love each other" (John 15:17). "So now I am giving you a new commandment: Love each other. Just as I have loved you, you should love each other. [35]Your love for one another will prove to the world that you are my disciples" (John 13:34-35).

O—Obedience. We will obey His commands. "If you love me, obey my commandments" (John 14:15).

C—Commitment. Disciples are willing to pay the price of following Christ. "The truth is, a kernel of wheat must be planted in the soil. Unless it dies it will be alone—a single seed. But its death will produce many new kernels—a plentiful harvest of new lives. [25]Those who love their life in this world will lose it. Those who despise their life in this world will keep it for eternal life. [26]All those who want to be my disciples must come and follow me, because my servants must be where I am. And if they follow me, the Father will honor them" (John 12:24-26).

K—Keeping. Disciples stay connected to Christ. "Remain in me, and I will remain in you. For a branch cannot produce fruit if it is severed from the vine, and you cannot be fruitful apart from me. [5]Yes, I am the vine; you are the branches. Those who remain in me, and I in them, will produce much fruit. For apart from me you can do nothing" (John 15:4 & 5).

S—Serving. Disciples follow the example of Christ who came to serve others. He washed the feet of the apostles the night before He made the ultimate sacrifice. "So he got up from the table, took off his robe, wrapped a towel around his waist, [5]and poured water into a basin. Then he began to wash the disciples' feet and to wipe them with the towel he had around him" (John 13:4-5).

When a flock of disciples reflects the pattern Jesus set for them, they will produce "fruit" (spiritual growth).

"My true disciples produce much fruit. This brings great glory to my Father" (John 15:8).

Flocks witness!

Be Filled with the Spirit

A third pattern for fully experiencing a holy life which is pleasing to God is consistently walking in the Spirit by being filled with the Spirit, or yielding to Him.

We can take steps that will draw us closer to God's will for our lives and will enrich us. To do this it helps to look at the goal from God's perspective. Let's look at some related passages on the subject.

"So be careful how you live, not as fools but as those who are wise. [16]Make the most of every opportunity for doing good in these evil days. [17]Don't act thoughtlessly, but try to understand what the Lord wants you to do. [18]Don't be drunk with wine, because that will ruin your life. Instead, *let the Holy Spirit fill and control you.* [19]Then you will sing psalms and hymns and spiritual songs among yourselves, making music to the Lord in your hearts. [20]And you will always give thanks for everything to God the Father in the name of our Lord Jesus Christ. [21]And further, you will submit to one another out of reverence for Christ" (Ephesians 5:15-21).

The main thought in this passage is to "let the Holy Spirit fill and control you." As a result, we will do several things. First, we will sing songs and hymns to each other. The words out of our months should be words of encouragement, words that always build up and never tear down. If we speak to each other this way, our relationships will be better.

Second, we will have music and a melody in our hearts. That's joy. That's emotional well-being. When we know, understand, and feel that God meets all our deepest needs, we are joyful people, from the inside out, not dependent on our circumstances.

Third, we will always be giving thanks to God in the name of Christ for everything. How often? All the time. For how much will we give thanks? Everything. When we dwell on what Christ did for us, how can we be anything but grateful? How can we do anything but praise Him? Things may not be great for us all the time here on the earth, but they could be much worse. We could have gotten what we really deserve, public execution on a cross, eternal separation from God and eternal damnation and excruciating pain in the fires of hell forever. We should be eternally grateful.

Fourth, we will serve one another out of reverence for Christ, who served us. Husbands are to serve their wives as

Christ served the church in love and gave up His life for us. That means putting a wife first as reflected in a husband's time, checkbook, mind, and heart. Wives are to respect their husbands and serve them as helpmates, not critics. All of us are to serve one another. This is the basis of common courtesy, putting the other person first, and demonstrating the unconditional love of God through your attitude toward other people.

The results of being filled with the Holy Spirit sound glorious. A song in your heart. Joyful relationships. Praising God and giving thanks. Everyone loving and serving one another.

This all sounds great, but what does it mean to be filled and controlled by the Spirit. How do I do this?

Note Colossians 3:15-17, a passage similar to Ephesians 5:15-21.

"And let the peace that comes from Christ rule in your hearts. For as members of one body you are all called to live in peace. And always be thankful.

[16]"Let the words of Christ, in all their richness, live in your hearts and make you wise. Use his words to teach and counsel each other. Sing psalms and hymns and spiritual songs to God with thankful hearts. [17]And whatever you do or say, let it be as a representative of the Lord Jesus, all the while giving thanks through him to God the Father."

This passage points to the same outcomes as the passage from Ephesians. We'll have peace, joy, thankfulness in our hearts, singing psalms and hymns, teaching and helping one another.

Whereas Ephesians 5:18 tells us to be filled with the Spirit, Colossians 5:16 tells us to "let the words of Christ...live in your hearts." In other words, we are to be filled with the Word. Whether filled with the Spirit or the Word, the results are the same.

I don't understand *how* I can be filled by the Spirit. However, I can figure out how to be filled by the Word, the Bible. I can read it. I can listen to it being taught in church, from the pulpit, or a classroom. I can study it alone. I can meditate on it before I fall asleep. I can memorize parts of it. *I can be filled with the Word.*

"All Scripture is inspired by God and is useful to teach us what is true and to make us realize what is wrong in our lives. It straightens us out and teaches us to do what is right. ¹⁷It is God's way of preparing us in every way, fully equipped for every good thing God wants us to do" (2 Timothy 3:16-17).

Remember, all Scripture, with which we are to fill ourselves, is God-breathed. It teaches us what is the right path. It tells us when we've stepped off the right path. It gets us back on the right path and trains us to keep moving in the right direction. It guides us in our walk of faith. Why? So we will be prepared for every good thing God wants for us—a life of holiness—so we will experience His music, joy, peace, and good relationships.

Two Warning Verses

There are two dangers we should be aware of if we want to be filled with and controlled by the Spirit.

"Do not stifle the Holy Spirit," Paul warns in 1 Thessalonians 5:19. We can stifle or quench the Spirit if we resist His guidance in our lives. As noted earlier, the Holy Spirit is like our internal air traffic controller who helps guide us into safety. When we ignore or stifle His advice, we are asking for trouble. We are to yield the right of way in our lives to God the Holy Spirit.

The second warning from Paul is in Ephesians 4:30. *"And do not bring sorrow to God's Holy Spirit* by the way you live. Remember, he is the one who has identified you as his own, guaranteeing that you will be saved on the day of redemption."

Don't sorrow or grieve the Holy Spirit by the way you live. The process of sanctification involves a struggle between our old, depraved nature and our new, regenerated nature. Why would you want to crawl on the ground like a caterpillar when you can fly like a butterfly? Instead of living in accord with your old sin nature, turn away from your sins, repent, and walk on the right path.

Walk in the Spirit

Another suggestion to living as God wants you to is seen in Galatians 5:16-17. "So I advise you *to live* according to your new life in the Holy Spirit. Then you won't be doing what your sinful nature craves. [17]The old sinful nature loves to do evil, which is just opposite from what the Holy Spirit wants. And the Spirit gives us desires that are opposite from what the sinful nature desires. These two forces are constantly fighting each other, and your choices are never free from this conflict."

The New Living Translation and the New International Version both translate this passage using the word "live" in talking about the pattern for our new life. The Greek word is *peripateo*, which literally means "to walk." It's the same word Matthew and John used to describe Jesus walking on water.

If we could analyze walking with a slow-motion camera, we would see what a picture of faith the process is. One foot is up in the air, all our weight resting on the other, shifting with the next step. If our foot doesn't come down when and where expected, we'll fall. It actually takes time and practice to learn to walk, physically and spiritually. Once we've grown up some, the physical process of walking becomes second nature to us and we hardly think about it. We just do it. Learning to walk in faith, walking in the Spirit, is the same.

Sometimes God only gives us enough light on the path to see the next step. I used to hate that. I wanted to know what was ahead before I committed myself to the next step. I think it's only natural for us to want to know what's around the corner. But when you are walking by the Spirit, you are relying on the fact that *God* knows what's around the corner.

Walking in the Spirit is yielding control to God and taking one step at a time, trusting Him for the outcome. He knows what's ahead. He cares more about us than we care ourselves. He wants the best for us.

When the journey ahead looks too tough or too dangerous, beyond our comfort zone or ability to control, we tend to avoid taking the next step. We are afraid we might get run over by life if we don't stay in control. This is a conflict between self-control—our flesh or old nature—and Spirit control. How do you really walk in the Spirit when part of you is reluctant? We can face problems by taking baby steps. God is not asking you to run in the Spirit. I believe God honors our baby steps of faith. He'll continue to give you more light, and soon you'll be walking in the Spirit and it will be second nature to you, second nature to your new nature. Every step of faith we take builds more confidence in God so we can take even more steps.

Where can we find enough light to throw on the path for even that first baby step? Where do we find the light we need? Psalm 119:105 says, "Your word is a lamp for my feet and a light for my path."

Spend time in God's Word so you'll have a better opportunity to understand God's plan for you and how you can live a holy life. Listen to the guidance of the Holy Spirit, and do what He wants. Take a baby step if you need to. Learn to trust Him. Learn to walk in the Spirit.

Prayer

Part of living a holy life, dependent, and connected to the living God through the Lord Jesus Christ, is prayer. It has been said that even atheists pray when they are in trouble. Christians should pray as a normal and regular part of our lives.

"Pray at all times and on every occasion in the power of the Holy Spirit. Stay alert and be persistent in your prayers for all Christians everywhere" (Ephesians 6:18).

Prayer is simply talking to God. He talks to us today primarily through His Word, the Bible. We should be involved in both aspects of this communication to deepen our relationship and understanding.

Jesus prayed to God the Father and taught us how to pray. After ministering to multitudes of people and healing the sick, "The next day Jesus awoke long before daybreak and went out alone into the wilderness to pray" (Luke 1:35).

Jesus prayed for us, His disciples, as recorded in the beautiful prayer of John 17, Jesus' high priestly prayer. Read it often.

Jesus also said, "[7]When you pray, don't babble on and on as people of other religions do. They think their prayers are answered only by repeating their words again and again. [8]Don't be like them, because your Father knows exactly what you need even before you ask him! [9]Pray like this:

> Our Father in heaven,
>   may your name be honored.
> [10]May your Kingdom come soon.
>   May your will be done here on earth,
> just as it is in heaven.
>   [11]Give us our food for today,
> [12]and forgive us our sins,
>   just as we have forgiven those who have sinned
>   against us.
> [13]And don't let us yield to temptation,
>   but deliver us from the evil one"
>   (Matthew 6:7-13).

This should be called "The Disciples' Prayer" because Jesus was teaching us how to pray. How sad that many simply repeat the words of these verses again and again in direct violation of His teaching. Jesus was giving us a model prayer.

When I pray, I like to use an acrostic of the word GRACE.

G—Glorify God. We should pray to our heavenly Father. In doing so we glorify Him. Only God is worthy of prayer. Praise Him for who He is. Praise His attributes. We should pray for the coming of His kingdom—the fulfillment of His plan for the world—His will being done. Read some of the psalms to spur your imagination (especially Psalms 113-118 and 145-150.)

R—Repent. Confession is part of repentance. It means to agree with God that something is wrong and to turn away from it. Turn away from things in your life where you know you are being disobedient to God's will for you. Recognize what's wrong in your life and turn back toward God. (Read Daniel 9:4-23.)

A—Acknowledge His Grace by Thanking Him. Everything you have, your very life, is a gift from God. Be specific in thanking God for the ways He has already blessed you and demonstrated His faithfulness. (Read Psalm 116.)

C—Call on God. Ask Him to meet the needs of people in your life and your own needs. Yield your will to His. Be specific in your requests and petitions to the Lord.

Your heavenly Father delights in providing your food for today, your daily bread. As we pray in His will, which we can usually know from His Word and from the Holy Spirit who lives in us, we are blessed by knowing and accepting that He gives us what is best for us, that His will is what we truly want. (Read 1 John 5:13-15 and Psalm 86.)

E—Exalt the Lord. Elevate the name of the Lord Jesus Christ in whose name you pray. Praying in the name of Jesus is like taking His signed check to the bank of heaven. You do not have funds or credit there, but He does. (Read John 14:13 and 16:23-24.)

The result of prayer is the special peace that only God can provide.

"⁶Don't worry about anything; instead, pray about everything. Tell God what you need, and thank him for all he has done. ⁷If you do this, you will experience God's peace, which is far more wonderful than the human mind can understand. His peace will guard your hearts and minds as you live in Christ Jesus" (Philippians 4:6-7).

Make it your commitment to spend time in prayer and reading God's Word every day. It's a great way to start or end each day.

Chapter 13

Angels—Good and Bad

Angels have been a hot topic in the media for a number of years. At least one successful television series focuses on angels, and a number of movies deal with angels and demons. Do human beings get wings and become angels in the next life? Is Michael the archangel really the way he was portrayed by John Travolta as a beer-drinking womanizer? Was Al Pacino like the real Satan in "Devil's Advocate"?

Let's look at what the best authority on angels has to say about them. The Bible uses words in its original languages (*malak* in Hebrew and *angellos* in Greek), both of which mean "messenger." Angels are messengers with a ministry from God to people. All angels were created before the creation of the world, and they are distinct from all other created beings. Human beings never become angels. Angels are described as having the essential qualities of personality, including intelligence, moral will, emotions, and they can give intelligent worship to God. Angels are spiritual beings. They do not have bodies but they may appear as men. As angels are today they will be forever. At a time after they were created, some angels chose to obey God and some rebelled against Him. Since then, angels have been divided into two major categories, holy angels or good angels, also called elect angels, and fallen or bad angels, also called demons.

Holy Angels

Paul referred to "the holy angels" as witnesses, along with God and Jesus Christ (1 Timothy 5:21).

Only a few angels are named in the Bible. Michael the archangel is one. In a vision related in Daniel 10, a messenger from God told Daniel what Michael was doing at that time. "But for twenty-one days the spirit prince of the kingdom of Persia blocked my way.

Then Michael, one of the archangels, came to help me, and I left him there with the spirit prince of the kingdom of Persia" (Daniel 10:13). Then Daniel reported that these good angels struggled with what seems to be a bad angel, "the spirit prince" of Persia. In Daniel 12:1 we read, "At that time Michael, the archangel who stands guard over your nation [Israel], will arise."

In Revelation 12:7-8 the fall from heaven of the bad angels is described. "Then there was war in heaven. Michael and the angels under his command fought the dragon and his angels. [8]And the dragon lost the battle and was forced out of heaven."

Another angel mentioned by name is Gabriel. Daniel's vision about the future was explained to him by Gabriel. "As Gabriel approached the place where I was standing, I became so terrified that I fell to the ground. 'Son of man,' he said, 'you must understand that the events you have seen in your vision relate to the time of the end'" (Daniel 8:17).

Gabriel then explained the meaning of the vision as it related to the future time coming for Israel and the world, the seventy sets of seven, the coming of the Messiah, and the Tribulation in Daniel 9:21-27. Gabriel is also the one who announced the coming birth of John the Baptist to his father and the birth of Jesus to Mary, as related in Luke 1:11-38.

What Do Angels Look Like?

The greatest description of a supernatural appearance by angels may be from the prophet Ezekiel, as he described the time when God commissioned him.

"On July 31 of my thirtieth year, while I was with the Judean exiles beside the Kebar River in Babylon, the heavens were opened to me, and I saw visions of God. [2]This happened during the fifth year of King Jehoiachin's captivity. [3]The LORD gave a message to me, Ezekiel son of Buzi, a priest, there beside the Kebar River in the land of the Babylonians, and I felt the hand of the LORD take hold of me.

[4]"As I looked, I saw a great storm coming toward me from the north, driving before it a huge cloud that flashed with lightning and shone with brilliant light. The fire inside the cloud glowed like gleaming amber. [5]From the center of the cloud came four living beings that looked human, [6]except that each had four faces and two pairs of wings. [7]Their legs were straight like human legs, but their feet were split like calves' feet and shone like burnished bronze. [8]Beneath each of their wings I could see human hands. [9]The wings of each living being touched the wings of the two beings beside it. The living beings were able to fly in any direction without turning around. [10]Each had a human face in the front, the face of a lion on the right side, the face of an ox on the left side, and the face of an eagle at the back. [11]Each had two pairs of outstretched wings—one pair stretched out to touch the wings of the living beings on either side of it, and the other pair covered its body. [12]They went in whatever direction the spirit chose, and they moved straight forward in all directions without having to turn around.

[13]"The living beings looked like bright coals of fire or brilliant torches, and it looked as though lightning was flashing back and forth among them. [14]And the living beings darted to and fro like flashes of lightning.

¹⁵"As I looked at these beings, I saw four wheels on the ground beneath them, one wheel belonging to each. ¹⁶The wheels sparkled as if made of chrysolite. All four wheels looked the same; each wheel had a second wheel turning crosswise within it. ¹⁷The beings could move forward in any of the four directions they faced, without turning as they moved. ¹⁸The rims of the four wheels were awesomely tall, and they were covered with eyes all around the edges. ¹⁹When the four living beings moved, the wheels moved with them. When they flew upward, the wheels went up, too. ²⁰The spirit of the four living beings was in the wheels. So wherever the spirit went, the wheels and the living beings went, too. ²¹When the living beings moved, the wheels moved. When the living beings stopped, the wheels stopped. When the living beings flew into the air, the wheels rose up. For the spirit of the living beings was in the wheels.

²²"There was a surface spread out above them like the sky. It sparkled like crystal. ²³Beneath this surface the wings of each living being stretched out to touch the others' wings, and each had two wings covering its body. ²⁴As they flew their wings roared like waves crashing against the shore, or like the voice of the Almighty, or like the shouting of a mighty army. When they stopped, they let down their wings. ²⁵As they stood with their wings lowered, a voice spoke from beyond the crystal surface above them.

²⁶"Above the surface over their heads was what looked like a throne made of blue sapphire. And high above this throne was a figure whose appearance was like that of a man. ²⁷From his waist up, he looked like gleaming amber, flickering like a fire. And from his waist down, he looked like a burning flame, shining with splendor. ²⁸All around him was a glowing halo, like a rainbow shining through the clouds. This was the way the glory of the LORD appeared to me. When I saw it, I fell face down in the dust, and I heard someone's voice speaking to me. 'Stand up son of man,' said the voice. 'I want to speak with you.' The Spirit came into me

as he spoke and set me on my feet. I listened carefully to his words" (Ezekiel 1:1-2:2).

In chapters nine and ten, Ezekiel identifies these angels as cherabim, apparently a kind of angel.

When Isaiah was commissioned by God, he saw seraphim, another kind of angel. "In the year King Uzziah died, I saw the Lord. He was sitting on a lofty throne, and the train of his robe filled the Temple. ²Hovering around him were mighty seraphim, each with six wings. With two wings they covered their faces, with two they covered their feet, and with the remaining two they flew. ³In a great chorus they sang, 'Holy, holy, holy is the LORD Almighty! The whole earth is filled with his glory!' ⁴The glorious singing shook the Temple to its foundations, and the entire sanctuary was filled with smoke.

⁵"Then I said, 'My destruction is sealed, for I am a sinful man and a member of a sinful race. Yet I have seen the King, the LORD Almighty!'

⁶"Then one of the seraphim flew over to the altar, and he picked up a burning coal with a pair of tongs. ⁷He touched my lips with it and said, 'See, this coal has touched your lips. Now your guilt is removed, and your sins are forgiven.'

⁸"Then I heard the Lord asking, 'Whom should I send as a messenger to my people? Who will go for us?' And I said, 'Lord, I'll go! Send me'" (Isaiah 6:1-8).

The Angel of the Lord

There are many Old Testament references to the Angel of the Lord or the Angel of Yahweh, a messenger from God. Biblical scholars have two opinions on his identity. Some say he is another high-ranking angel like Michael or Gabriel. Others say he is the preincarnate Christ. He appeared to Moses in the burning bush and then identified himself as God.

"One day Moses was tending the flock of his fa-
ther-in-law, Jethro, the priest of Midian, and he went deep
into the wilderness near Sinai, the mountain of God.
²Suddenly, the angel of the LORD appeared to him as a blazing fire in a bush. Moses was amazed because the bush was
engulfed in flames, but it didn't burn up. ³'Amazing!' Moses
said to himself. 'Why isn't that bush burning up? I must go
over to see this.'

⁴"When the LORD saw that he had caught Moses' attention, God called to him from the bush, 'Moses! Moses!'

"'Here I am!' Moses replied.

⁵"'Do not come any closer,' God told him. 'Take off your
sandals, for you are standing on holy ground.' ⁶Then he said,
'I am the God of your ancestors—the God of Abraham, the
God of Isaac, and the God of Jacob.' When Moses heard this,
he hid his face in his hands because he was afraid to look at
God" (Exodus 3:1-6).

The angel of the Lord is also identified as God when he
appeared to Gideon. See Judges 6:11-24.

The Lord Jesus Christ could have been referred to as an
angel because He did come as a messenger with a ministry
from God to people. These preincarnation appearances of
Christ, the second person of the Godhead, the Angel of
Yahweh, are called "theophanies." The first and third persons of the Godhead are never revealed physically. The Angel of Yahweh never appears after the physical birth of
Jesus.

Guardian Angels

Do people have guardian angels?

When the King of Aram sent an army to seize the prophet
Elisha, Elisha calmed his servant who was frightened by say-
ing that the "troops, horse, and chariots [are] everywhere.
'Ah, my Lord, what will we do now?' he cried out to Elisha.

'Don't be afraid!' Elisha told him. 'For there are more on our side than on theirs!' [17]Then Elisha prayed, 'O LORD , open his eyes and let him see!' The LORD opened his servant's eyes, and when he looked up, he saw that the hillside around Elisha was filled with horses and chariots of fire" (2 Kings 6:15-17).

A psalmist wrote, "[11]For he orders his angels to protect you wherever you go. [12]They will hold you with their hands to keep you from striking your foot on a stone" (Psalm 91:9-16).

In the New Testament, the apostles were rescued by an angel of the Lord after the high priest had them arrested. "But an angel of the Lord came at night, opened the gates of the jail, and brought them out" (Acts 5:18-19). Later Peter was again miraculously rescued from prison by an angel (Acts 12:6-11).

The Work of Holy Angels

According to the Bible holy angels have two primary duties. The first is that they worship God.

"In front of the throne was a shiny sea of glass, sparkling like crystal. In the center and around the throne were four living beings, each covered with eyes, front and back. [7]The first of these living beings had the form of a lion; the second looked like an ox; the third had a human face; and the fourth had the form of an eagle with wings spread out as though in flight. [8]Each of these living beings had six wings, and their wings were covered with eyes, inside and out. Day after day and night after night they keep on saying, 'Holy, holy, holy is the Lord God Almighty—the one who always was, who is, and who is still to come'" (Revelation 4:6-8).

The other primary duty of holy angels is to perform tasks for God. They protect believers as guardian angels, as we have already noted. They provide guidance to believers, even if we don't recognize where this guidance is coming from. Angels were at the empty tomb after the resurrection to tell the disciples Jesus had risen (Matthew 28:5-7). In the Book of Daniel we saw their role in restraining and guiding nations and as God's agents in answering prayer. Angels also help bring God's judgment against evil, as seen in Revelation 16.

Show Hospitality to Angels

Good angels seem to watch over us, protect us, and witness our activities. The author of Hebrews reminds us of this. "Don't forget to show hospitality to strangers, for some who have done this have entertained angels without realizing it" (Hebrews 13:2).

Fallen Angels, Evil Spirits, or Demons

Some fallen angels are bound, and some are not. They are called demons or evil spirits.

"For God did not spare even the angels when they sinned; he threw them into hell, in gloomy caves and darkness until the judgment day" (2 Peter 2:4).

"And I remind you of the angels who did not stay within the limits of authority God gave them but left the place where they belonged. God has kept them chained in prisons of darkness, waiting for the day of judgment" (Jude 6).

Some evil spirits, fallen angels or demons, are still free to roam the earth. In Mark 5:1-20, we see Jesus dealing with many evil spirits who had possessed a man.

"So they arrived at the other side of the lake, in the land of the Gerasenes. ²Just as Jesus was climbing from the boat, a man possessed by an evil spirit ran out from a cemetery to meet him. ³This man lived among the tombs and could not be restrained, even with a chain. ⁴Whenever he was put into chains and shackles—as he often was—he snapped the chains from his wrists and smashed the shackles. No one was strong enough to control him. [5]All day long and throughout the night, he would wander among the tombs and in the hills, screaming and hitting himself with stones.

[6]"When Jesus was still some distance away, the man saw him. He ran to meet Jesus and fell down before him. [7]He gave a terrible scream, shrieking, 'Why are you bothering me, Jesus, Son of the Most High God? For God's sake, don't torture me!' [8]For Jesus had already said to the spirit, 'Come out of the man, you evil spirit.'

[9]"Then Jesus asked, 'What is your name?'

"And the spirit replied, 'Legion, because there are many of us here inside this man.' [10]Then the spirits begged him again and again not to send them to some distant place. [11]There happened to be a large herd of pigs feeding on the hillside nearby. [12]'Send us into those pigs,' the evil spirits begged. [13]Jesus gave them permission. So the evil spirits came out of the man and entered the pigs, and the entire herd of two thousand pigs plunged down the steep hillside into the lake, where they drowned.

[14]"The herdsmen fled to the nearby city and the surrounding countryside, spreading the news as they ran. Everyone rushed out to see for themselves. [15]A crowd soon gathered around Jesus, but they were frightened when they saw the man who had been demon possessed, for he was sitting there fully clothed and perfectly sane. [16]Those who had seen what happened to the man and to the pigs told everyone about it, [17]and the crowd began pleading with Jesus to go away and leave them alone.

[18]"When Jesus got back into the boat, the man who had been demon possessed begged to go, too. [19]But Jesus said, 'No, go home to your friends, and tell them what wonderful things the Lord has done for you and how merciful he has been.' [20]So the man started off to visit the Ten Towns of that region and began to tell everyone about the great things

Jesus had done for him; and everyone was amazed at what he told them" (Mark 5:1-20).

"Now the Holy Spirit tells us clearly that in the last times some will turn away from what we believe; they will follow lying spirits and teachings that come from demons" (1 Timothy 4:1).

All the fallen angels are called this because they fell from heaven. "Then there was war in heaven. Michael and the angels under his command fought the dragon and his angels. [8]And the dragon lost the battle and was forced out of heaven. [9]This great dragon—the ancient serpent called the Devil, or Satan, the one deceiving the whole world—was thrown down to the earth with all his angels" (Revelation 12:7-9).

All of the fallen angels are doomed. "Then the King will turn to those on the left and say, 'Away with you, you cursed ones, into the eternal fire prepared for the Devil and his demons" (Matthew 25:41).

Satan or the Devil

The devil, or Satan, is the only fallen angel named in the Bible. He is a person, not some evil force or principle. The Bible tells us Satan was created above all other creatures, but he sinned against God.

The prophet Ezekiel was given a message from the Lord about Satan. He is referred to as the king of Tyre, a wicked king under Satan's control at the time, but it is impossible for any man to be described this way. The passage is talking about Satan.

"Then this further message came to me from the LORD: [12]'Son of man, weep for the king of Tyre. Give him this message from the Sovereign LORD: *You were the perfection of wisdom and beauty.* [13]You were in Eden, the garden of God. Your clothing was adorned with every precious stone—red carnelian, chrysolite, white moonstone, beryl, onyx, jasper, sapphire, turquoise, and emerald—all beautifully crafted for you and set in the finest gold. They were given to you on the day you were created. [14]I ordained and anointed you as the mighty angelic guardian. You had access to the holy mountain of God and walked among the stones of fire.

[15]"'You were blameless in all you did from the day you were created until the day evil was found in you. [16]Your great wealth filled you with violence, and you sinned. So I banished you from the mountain of God. I expelled you, O mighty guardian, from your place among the stones of fire. [17]Your heart was filled with pride because of all your beauty. You corrupted your wisdom for the sake of your splendor. So I threw you to the earth and exposed you to the curious gaze of kings. [18]You defiled your sanctuaries with your many sins and your dishonest trade. So I brought fire from within you, and it consumed you. I let it burn you to ashes on the ground in the sight of all who were watching. [19]All who knew you are appalled at your fate. You have come to a terrible end, and you are no more'" (Ezekiel 28:11-19).

This passage describes the terrible fall of Satan, even though the final events have not yet taken place.

In verse 12 Satan is described as the "perfection of wisdom and beauty." This led to Satan's pride and wickedness. The same can happen to human beings who become full of themselves.

Satan's rebellion is also detailed by the prophet Isaiah.

"How you are fallen from heaven, O shining star, son of the morning! You have been thrown down to the earth, you who destroyed the nations of the world. [13]For you said to yourself, '*I will* ascend to heaven and set my throne above God's stars. *I will* preside on the mountain of the gods far away in the north. [14]*I will* climb to the highest heavens and be like the Most High.' [15]But instead, you will be brought down to the place of the dead, down to its lowest depths. [16]Everyone there will stare at you and ask, 'Can this be the one who shook the earth and the kingdoms of the world? [17]Is this the one who destroyed the world and made it into a wilderness? Is this the king who demolished the world's greatest cities and had no mercy on his prisoners?'" (Isaiah 14:12-17).

In his prideful wickedness Satan wanted to be like God, and so he tried to usurp God's authority in heaven. He was defeated and cast down with those angels who followed him.

Here are other ways Satan is described.

Revelation 20:10 refers to "the Devil, who betrayed them." He is a betrayer and deceiver. He cannot be trusted under any circumstances.

"For you are the children of your father the Devil, and you love to do the evil things he does. He was a murderer from the beginning and has always hated the truth. There is no truth in him. When he lies, it is consistent with his character; for he is a liar and the father of lies" (John 8:44). He is a liar and a murderer.

His deceptive nature is seen in that he "can disguise himself as an angel of light" (2 Corinthians 11:14). In fact he seeks to deceive "the whole world" (Revelation 12:9).

Satan is also called the Accuser (Revelation 12:10), and he has access to God, according to the Book of Job. "One day the angels came to present themselves before the Lord, and Satan the Accuser came with them. 'Where have you come from?' the Lord asked Satan. And Satan answered the Lord, 'I have been going back and forth across the earth, watching everything that's going on'" (Job 1:6-7).

He also has access to people, as the apostle Peter warned. "Be careful! Watch out for attacks from the Devil, your great enemy. He prows around like a roaring lion, looking for some victim to devour" (1 Peter 5:8).

Believers need not become the devil's victims. We can deal with him by resisting him. "So humble yourselves before God. Resist the Devil, and he will flee from you" (James 4:7).

We can respect Satan's power, but we need not respect his authority.

Satan's Work Today

He has possession of the unsaved. They are his "prisoners," according to Isaiah 13:17. As Paul wrote in Ephesians 2:1-2, "Once you were dead, doomed forever because of your many sins. ²You used to live just like the rest of the world, full of sin, obeying Satan, the mighty prince of the power of the air. He is the spirit at work in the hearts of those who refuse to obey God." But Christ has saved believers. "For he has rescued us from the one who rules in the kingdom of darkness" (Colossians 1:13).

Practical Life Application

Christians can stop Satan by putting on the armor of God.

"A final word: Be strong with the Lord's mighty power. ¹¹Put on all of God's armor so that you will be able to stand firm against all strategies and tricks of the Devil. ¹²For we are not fighting against people made of flesh and blood, but against the evil rulers and authorities of the unseen world, against those mighty powers of darkness who rule this world, and against wicked spirits in the heavenly realms.

¹³"Use every piece of God's armor to resist the enemy in the time of evil, so that after the battle you will still be standing firm. ¹⁴Stand your ground, putting on the sturdy belt of truth and the body armor of God's righteousness. ¹⁵For shoes, put on the peace that comes from the Good News, so that you will be fully prepared. ¹⁶In every battle you will need faith as your shield to stop the fiery arrows aimed at

you by Satan. [17]Put on salvation as your helmet, and take the sword of the Spirit, which is the word of God. [18]Pray at all times and on every occasion in the power of the Holy Spirit. Stay alert and be persistent in your prayers for all Christians everywhere" (Ephesians 6:10-18).

We also know Satan will create false religions to deceive people. "But I fear that somehow you will be led away from your pure and simple devotion to Christ, just as Eve was deceived by the serpent. [4]You seem to believe whatever anyone tells you, even if they preach about a different Jesus than the one we preach, or a different Spirit than the one you received, or a different kind of gospel than the one you believed....These people are false apostles. They have fooled you by disguising themselves as apostles of Christ. [14]But I am not surprised! Even Satan can disguise himself as an angel of light. [15]So it is no wonder his servants can also do it by pretending to be godly ministers. In the end they will get every bit of punishment their wicked deeds deserve" (2 Corinthians 11:3-4; 13-15).

Most false religions claiming to be Christian fall into one of three categories. They preach a different Jesus, not the God-Man of the Bible. As we discussed in the section on the person of Jesus Christ, he had to be fully man to substitute for us and He had to be fully God in order to forgive us. Or second, they preach a different Spirit, one that calls attention to himself instead of Jesus, thus causing confusion instead of unity in the body. Or third, they preach a message that adds something to faith as the requirement for salvation. When ice melts in a glass of Coca Cola, it is no longer refreshing. It is no longer the real thing. When you dilute the gospel by adding something to it, you do not have the gospel by which we are saved, as written in 1 Corinthians 15 or John 3:16.

Satan was thrown out of heaven, and one day he will be thrown into the lake of fire for eternal punishment. Christ won the victory at the cross and His resurrection! We win! If

Satan tries to discourage you by bringing up your past, remind him of his future.

Chapter 14

Things Still To Come

From the very beginning God has had a plan for the world. Nothing has changed His plan, and nothing will. From our creation, to our rebellion and fall, including the eternal punishment of the rebels and the salvation of some through the Lord Jesus Christ, He is the Sovereign of the universe.

Three Ways to View the Future

Christians have been divided over their views of interpreting the Bible as it pertains to the future of the world. The key term in the argument is the word "millennium," which means "thousand" and has to do with the return of Christ.

Amillennialists believe in a spiritual interpretation and reject a literal thousand-year reign on earth. The kingdom promises to Israel are viewed symbolically or as fulfilled in the church through Christ's spiritual reign in the hearts of believers. Augustine's embrace of amillennialism in the fifth century has dominated church thought since then. When Christ had not returned after hundreds of years, Christians came to think they had misunderstood the teachings about His return. So they abandoned the literal interpretation of biblical prophecy and began the difficult process of spiritualizing parts of the Bible. In spiritualizing the Bible, liberal theologians think they can make the Bible mean anything they want to.

Postmillennialists expect the church to triumphantly Christianize the world into a one-thousand-year golden age that will climax with the return of Christ. This school of thought peaked after the Enlightenment and the advance of civilization into the twentieth century. The reality of two world wars and the rise of brutal, totalitarian governments in Nazi Germany and communist Russia and China disillusioned many postmillennialists. It has made something of a comeback with reconstructionists in America, who hope to impose their religious views on society in general.

Premillennialists, believing in a literal or natural interpretation of all Scripture, see the thousand years as a literal period of time with the Lord Christ reigning over the entire world from His throne in Jerusalem. Consistent with its interpretation, premillennialism sees a seven-year period of tribulation coming on the world prior to the return of Christ to set up His kingdom. Since the 1830s the premillennialists have been led by Bible teachers like John Darby, D. L. Moody, C. I. Scofield, Lewis Sperry Chafer, Charles C. Ryrie, John F. Walvoord, J. Dwight Pentecost, and Charles Swindoll.

Some of the key verses dealing with Christ's kingdom include the following.

"For the LORD declares, 'I have placed my chosen king on the throne in Jerusalem, my holy city.' [7]The king proclaims the LORD's decree: 'The LORD said to me, "You are my son. Today I have become your Father. [8]Only ask, and I will give you the nations as your inheritance, the ends of the earth as your possession"'" (Psalm 2:6-8).

"In that day the wolf and the lamb will live together; the leopard and the goat will be at peace.... In that day the heir to David's throne will be a banner of salvation to all the world. The nations will rally to him, for the land where he lives will be a glorious place. [11]In that day the Lord will bring back a remnant of his people for the second time, returning them to the land of Israel from Assyria, Lower Egypt, Upper Egypt, Ethiopia, Elam, Babylonia, Hamath, and all the distant coastlands" (Isaiah 11:6, 10-11).

Revelation 20 uses the phrase "thousand years" six times and depicts the resurrected saints of the church and those believers killed in the Tribulation as reigning "with Christ for a thousand years. ...they will be priests of God and Christ and will reign with him a thousand years" (Revelation 20: 4, 6).

None of these prophecies has yet been fulfilled. If God is God, when He makes a promise it must come true. Since it has not happened yet, it must be coming to fulfillment at sometime in the future. We can count on that.

Understanding World History
Through Three Kinds of People

The Bible divides people into three kinds: Israelites or Jewish people; members of the church, those called Christians, both Jewish and Gentile; and Gentiles.

1. The people of Israel are God's chosen people. They had special, divine revelation, including the Law. They also had special dealings with God, including the promise of a deliverer, their Messiah. A timetable was set in motion for Israel, which has not yet been completed.

"A period of seventy sets of seven has been decreed for your people and your holy city to put down rebellion, to bring an end to sin, to atone for guilt, to bring in everlasting righteousness, to confirm the prophetic vision, and to anoint the Most Holy Place. [25]Now listen and understand! Seven sets of seven plus sixty-two sets of seven will pass from the time the command is given to rebuild Jerusalem until the

Anointed One comes. Jerusalem will be rebuilt with streets and strong defenses, despite the perilous times.

[26]"After this period of sixty-two sets of seven, the Anointed One will be killed, appearing to have accomplished nothing, and a ruler will arise whose armies will destroy the city and the Temple. The end will come with a flood, and war and its miseries are decreed from that time to the very end. [27]He will make a treaty with the people for a period of one set of seven, but after half this time, he will put an end to the sacrifices and offerings. Then as a climax to all his terrible deeds, he will set up a sacrilegious object that causes desecration, until the end that has been decreed is poured out on this defiler" (Daniel 9:24-27).

In the chapter on dispensations we discussed this passage. Seventy sets of seven, each set meaning a period of seven years, or 490 total, were decreed for Israel from the rebuilding of the city after the Babylonian destruction.

Seven plus sixty-two sets (483 years) occurred before the Anointed One came. This period of time extended from the date of the decree to the time Christ entered Jerusalem on what we call Palm Sunday, a week before He was killed. That leaves one more set, or seven years, on Israel's timetable. This timetable was suspended during the Church Age, which Christ, the rejected Messiah, inaugurated after His resurrection.

Daniel wrote this about six hundred years before Christ, after Daniel had been taken off to Babylon.

2. The church was a mystery not revealed by God until the time of Christ and His rejection by Israel as its Messiah. The church, all born-again Christians, also has special revelation from God, including the New Testament. Church believers also have the indwelling of the Holy Spirit and grace as the mode by which we are to live.

3. Gentiles include all unbelieving non-Jewish people. God demonstrates His sovereignty and omnipotence over all world history. Even though Israel and the church are set apart from world history or the history of the Gentiles, we are all part of one story and God is the author.

"And Jerusalem will be conquered and trampled down by the Gentiles until the age of the Gentiles comes to an end" (Luke 21:24).

Other passages that are key to understanding Gentile and Jewish world history are found in Daniel 2, 7, and 8.

Daniel interpreted King Nebuchadnezzar's dream of an image, and God gave Daniel a vision of four ruling nations from the Gentile world. Nebuchadnezzar's Babylon would be replaced by the Persian Empire. Then Greece under Alexander the Great would sweep across the world. Finally, Rome would rule the world, eventually through a confederation of states making up the Roman Empire. The last king of the Roman confederation is the one Daniel later called the "defiler" in Daniel 9:27. His demise or end will occur before the Messiah sets up His kingdom in Jerusalem.

The stage is set. We have seven more years on Israel's clock, a time of great trouble. When will it start ticking again?

What Next?

Let's outline the major events still to come in God's prophetic program for the world. This program can be divided into two parts. The first, which has been called the Day of Christ, involves only the church and most of the activity takes place in heaven. The second part, which is known as the Day of the Lord, takes place on earth. It focuses on the people of Israel and the Gentiles.

The Church

1.   Resurrection of the dead in Christ and

2.   Rapture of the saints alive on earth who are taken to heaven

"But let me tell you a wonderful secret God has revealed to us. Not all of us will die, but we will all be transformed. [52]It will happen in a moment, in the blinking of an eye, when the last trumpet is blown. For when the trumpet sounds, the Christians who have died will be raised with transformed bodies. And then we who are living will be transformed so that we will never die. [53]For our perishable earthly bodies must be transformed into heavenly bodies that will never die" (1 Corinthians 15:51-53).

"And now, brothers and sisters, I want you to know what will happen to the Christians who have died so you will not be full of sorrow like people who have no hope. [14]For since we believe that Jesus died and was raised to life again, we also believe that when Jesus comes, God will bring back with Jesus all the Christians who have died.

[15]"I can tell you this directly from the Lord: We who are still living when the Lord returns will not rise to meet him ahead of those who are in their graves. [16]For the Lord himself will come down from heaven with a commanding shout, with the call of the archangel, and with the trumpet call of God. First, all the Christians who have died will rise from their graves. [17]Then, together with them, we who are still alive and remain on the earth will be caught up in the clouds to meet the Lord in the air and remain with him forever. [18]So comfort and encourage each other with these words" (1 Thessalonians 4:13-18).

Many Christians believe the rapture of the saints will take place just before the start of the seven year tribulation on earth. Others believe the rapture will occur during the tribulation just before the full wrath of God is poured out on the world. In either case, we are to be ready.

3.　Bema Seat Awards Ceremony

"For we must all stand before Christ to be judged. We will each receive whatever we deserve for the good or evil we have done in our bodies" (2 Corinthians 5:10).

"So why do you condemn another Christian? Why do you look down on another Christian? Remember, each of us will stand personally before the judgment seat of God. [11]For the Scriptures say, 'As surely as I live,' says the Lord, 'every knee will bow to me and every tongue will confess allegiance to God.' [12]Yes, each of us will have to give a personal account to God" (Romans 14:10-12).

"As for me, my life has already been poured out as an offering to God. The time of my death is near. [7]I have fought a good fight, I have finished the race, and I have remained faithful. [8]And now the prize awaits me—the crown of righteousness that the Lord, the righteous Judge, will give me on that great day of his return. And the prize is not just for me but for all who eagerly look forward to his glorious return" (2 Timothy 4:6-8).

The "Bema" or "Judgment Seat of Christ" has been likened to a medal ceremony at the Olympics. Not everyone gets a medal. Only the top finishers are given special honors. At the Bema, some will be rewarded for their faithfulness. But like the Olympics, everyone else will still be glad to be there. After all, we don't take the fourth place finishers in Olympic events and shoot them. Of course not. They are still honored champions in their own countries.

The sins of believers were judged at the Cross. At the Judgment Seat of Christ our service and motives will be evaluated.

4.   The Wedding Feast of the Lamb and His Bride (the Church)

"Then I heard again what sounded like the shout of a huge crowd, or the roar of mighty ocean waves, or the crash of loud thunder: 'Hallelujah! For the Lord our God, the Almighty, reigns. [7]Let us be glad and rejoice and honor him. For the time has come for the wedding feast of the Lamb, and his bride has prepared herself. [8]She is permitted to wear the finest white linen.' (Fine linen represents the good deeds done by the people of God.)

[9]"And the angel said, 'Write this: Blessed are those who are invited to the wedding feast of the Lamb.' And he added, 'These are true words that come from God'" (Revelation 19:6-9).

5.   Return with Christ to Serve and Reign with Him

"Then I saw heaven opened, and a white horse was standing there. And the one sitting on the horse was named Faithful and True. For he judges fairly and then goes to war. [12]His eyes were bright like flames of fire, and on his head were many crowns. A name was written on him, and only he knew what it meant. [13]He was clothed with a robe dipped in blood, and his title was the Word of God. [14]The armies of heaven, dressed in pure white linen, followed him on white horses. [15]From his mouth came a sharp sword, and with it he struck down the nations. He ruled them with an iron rod, and he trod the winepress of the fierce wrath of almighty God. [16]On his robe and thigh was written this title: King of kings and Lord of lords" (Revelation 19:11-16).

Christ will establish His millennial kingdom and the church will serve Him there for one thousand years. While the church is in heaven preparing for this time, terrible things will be happening on earth with those left behind during that period of seven years.

Tribulation for the World

1. Rise of the new Roman confederation and its leader, the Antichrist

Passages from both the Old and New Testaments tell us of this prophecy. Daniel wrote about six hundred years before Christ. The apostle John wrote about seven hundred years later.

"Then in my vision that night, I saw a fourth beast, terrifying, dreadful, and very strong. It devoured and crushed its victims with huge iron teeth and trampled what was left beneath its feet. It was different from any of the other beasts, and it had ten horns. ⁸As I was looking at the horns, suddenly another small horn appeared among them. Three of the first horns were wrenched out, roots and all, to make room for it. This little horn had eyes like human eyes and a mouth that was boasting arrogantly" (Daniel 7:7-8).

"Then he said to me, 'This fourth beast is the fourth world power that will rule the earth. It will be different from all the others. It will devour the whole world, trampling everything in its path. ²⁴Its ten horns are ten kings that will rule that empire. Then another king will arise, different from the other ten, who will subdue three of them. ²⁵He will defy the Most High and wear down the holy people of the Most High. He will try to change their sacred festivals and laws, and they will be placed under his control for a time, times, and half a time'" (Daniel 7:23-25).

In chapter eight, Daniel recounts another vision he had with a ram and a goat that Gabriel explained to him.

"While he was speaking, I fainted and lay there with my face to the ground. But Gabriel roused me with a touch and helped me to my feet. ¹⁹Then he said, 'I am here to tell you what will happen later in the time of wrath. What you have seen pertains to the very end of time. ²⁰The two-horned ram represents the kings of Media and Persia. ²¹The shaggy male goat represents the king of Greece, and the large horn between its eyes represents the first king of the Greek Empire. [22]The four prominent horns that replaced the one large horn show that the Greek Empire will break into four sections with four kings, none of them as great as the first.

[23]"At the end of their rule, when their sin is at its height, a fierce king, a master of intrigue, will rise to power. [24]He will become very strong, but not by his own power. He will cause a shocking amount of destruction and succeed in everything he does. He will destroy powerful leaders and devastate the holy people. [25]He will be a master of deception, defeating many by catching them off guard. Without warning he will destroy them. He will even take on the Prince of princes in battle, but he will be broken, though not by human power'" (Daniel 8:18-25).

"After this period of sixty-two sets of seven, the Anointed One will be killed, appearing to have accomplished nothing, and a ruler will arise whose armies will destroy the city and the Temple. The end will come with a flood, and war and its miseries are decreed from that time to the very end. [27]He will make a treaty with the people for a period of one set of seven, but after half this time, he will put an end to the sacrifices and offerings. Then as a climax to all his terrible deeds, he will set up a sacrilegious object that causes desecration, until the end that has been decreed is poured out on this defiler" (Daniel 9:26-27).

"And now in my vision I saw a beast rising up out of the sea. It had seven heads and ten horns, with ten crowns on its horns. And written on each head were names that blasphemed God. [2]This beast looked like a leopard, but it had bear's feet and a lion's mouth! And the dragon gave him his own power and throne and great authority.

[3]"I saw that one of the heads of the beast seemed wounded beyond recovery—but the fatal wound was healed! All the world marveled at this miracle and followed the beast in awe. [4]They worshipped the dragon for giving the beast such power, and they worshipped the beast. 'Is

there anyone as great as the beast?' they exclaimed. 'Who is able to fight against him?'

[5]"Then the beast was allowed to speak great blasphemies against God. And he was given authority to do what he wanted for forty-two months. [6]And he spoke terrible words of blasphemy against God, slandering his name and all who live in heaven, who are his temple. [7]And the beast was allowed to wage war against God's holy people and to overcome them. And he was given authority to rule over every tribe and people and language and nation. [8]And all the people who belong to this world worshipped the beast. They are the ones whose names were not written in the Book of Life, which belongs to the Lamb who was killed before the world was made" (Revelation 13:1-8).

Daniel and John were talking about the rise and fall of kings and a world ruler who will make a peace treaty with Israel. After three and a half years he will break the treaty and will begin massive persecution of the Jewish people.

2. Signing of the seven-year peace treaty with Israel

"He will make a treaty with the people for a period of one set of seven, but after half this time, he will put an end to the sacrifices and offerings" (Daniel 9:27).

3. The Tribulation begins in which half the population of the earth will die

"Then there will be a time of anguish greater than any since nations first came into existence" (Daniel 12:1).

"For that will be a time of greater horror than anything the world has ever seen or will see again" (Matthew 24:21).

Revelation 6:8 says death will come to one-fourth of the earth. In Revelation 9:15-18 another third of those remaining will die.

4. The peace treaty is broken after three and a half years and the horror increases

"In all history there has never been such a time of terror. It will be a time of trouble for my people Israel. Yet in the end, they will be saved" (Jeremiah 30:7).

5. Two witnesses in the Tribulation are martyred in Jerusalem, resurrected, and taken to heaven

"And I will give power to my two witnesses, and they will be clothed in sackcloth and will prophesy during those 1,260 days.

[4]"These two prophets are the two olive trees and the two lampstands that stand before the Lord of all the earth. [5]If anyone tries to harm them, fire flashes from the mouths of the prophets and consumes their enemies. This is how anyone who tries to harm them must die. [6]They have power to shut the skies so that no rain will fall for as long as they prophesy. And they have the power to turn the rivers and oceans into blood, and to send every kind of plague upon the earth as often as they wish.

[7]"When they complete their testimony, the beast that comes up out of the bottomless pit will declare war against them. He will conquer them and kill them. [8]And their bodies will lie in the main street of Jerusalem, the city which is called 'Sodom' and 'Egypt,' the city where their Lord was crucified. [9]And for three and a half days, all peoples, tribes, languages, and nations will come to stare at their bodies. No one will be allowed to bury them. [10]All the people who belong to this world will give presents to each other to celebrate the death of the two prophets who had tormented them.

[11]But after three and a half days, the spirit of life from God entered them, and they stood up! And terror struck all who were staring at them. [12]Then a loud voice shouted from heaven, 'Come up here!' And they rose to heaven in a cloud as their enemies watched" (Revelation 11:3-12).

6. 144,000 Jewish evangelists preach the Gospel during the Tribulation

"And I heard how many were marked with the seal of God. There were 144,000 who were sealed from all the tribes of Israel" (Revelation7:4).

As God reclaims His chosen people, twelve thousand evangelists will be appointed for each of the twelve tribes of Israel.

7. Babylon and its allies attack Israel but their armies are destroyed

Ezekiel 38-39 discuss these events. Highlights are as follows.

"This is what the Sovereign LORD says: You are the one I was talking about long ago, when I announced through Israel's prophets that in future days I would bring you against my people. [18]But when Gog invades the land of Israel, says the Sovereign LORD , my fury will rise! [19]For in my jealousy and blazing anger, I promise a mighty shaking in the land of Israel on that day. [20]All living things—all the fish, birds, animals, and people—will quake in terror at my presence. Mountains will be thrown down; cliffs will crumble; walls will fall to the earth. [21]I will summon the sword against you throughout Israel, says the Sovereign LORD. Your men will turn against each other in mortal combat. [22]I will punish you and your hordes with disease and bloodshed; I will send torrential rain, hailstones, fire, and burning sulfur! [23]Thus will I show my greatness and holiness, and I will make myself known to all the nations of the world. Then they will know that I am the LORD!" (Ezekiel 38:17-23).

"And I will make a vast graveyard for Gog and his hordes in the Valley of the Travelers, east of the Dead Sea. The path of those who travel there will be blocked by this burial ground, and they will change the name of the place to the Valley of Gog's Hordes. [12]It will take seven months for the people of Israel to cleanse the land by burying the bodies. [13]Everyone in Israel will help, for it will be a glorious victory for Israel when I demonstrate my glory on that day, says the Sovereign LORD" (Ezekiel 39:11-13).

8. Babylon is destroyed

"After all this I saw another angel come down from heaven with great authority, and the earth grew bright with his splendor. [2]He gave a mighty shout, 'Babylon is fallen—that great city is fallen! She has become the hideout of demons and evil spirits, a nest for filthy buzzards, and a den for dreadful beasts. [3]For all the nations have drunk the wine of her passionate immorality. The rulers of the world have committed adultery with her, and merchants throughout the world have grown rich as a result of her luxurious living.'

[9]"And the rulers of the world who took part in her immoral acts and enjoyed her great luxury will mourn for her as they see the smoke rising from her charred remains. [10]They will stand at a distance, terrified by her great torment. They will cry out, 'How terrible, how terrible for Babylon, that great city! In one single moment God's judgment came on her'" (Revelation 18:1-3, 9-10).

9. The Antichrist gathers the armies of the world to fight against Christ at the Battle of Armageddon in Israel

"Then I saw the beast gathering the kings of the earth and their armies in order to fight against the one sitting on the horse and his army" (Revelation 19:19).

10. The Second Coming of Christ

"And then at last, the sign of the coming of the Son of Man will appear in the heavens, and there will be deep mourning among all the nations of the earth. And they will see the Son of Man arrive on the clouds of heaven with power and great glory. [31]And he will send forth his angels with the sound of a mighty trumpet blast, and they will gather together his chosen ones from the farthest ends of the earth and heaven" (Matthew 24:30-31).

"Then I saw heaven opened, and a white horse was standing there. And the one sitting on the horse was named Faithful and True. For he judges fairly and then goes to war. [12]His eyes were bright like flames of fire, and on his head were many crowns. A name was written on him, and only he knew what it meant. [13]He was clothed with a robe dipped in blood, and his title was the Word of God. [14]The armies of heaven, dressed in pure white linen, followed him on white horses. [15]From his mouth came a sharp sword, and with it he struck down the nations. He ruled them with an iron rod, and he trod the winepress of the fierce wrath of almighty God. [16]On his robe and thigh was written this title: King of kings and Lord of lords.

[17]"Then I saw an angel standing in the sun, shouting to the vultures flying high in the sky: 'Come! Gather together for the great banquet God has prepared. [18]Come and eat the flesh of kings, captains, and strong warriors; of horses and their riders; and of all humanity, both free and slave, small and great'" (Revelation 19:11-18).

11. The Antichrist and the false prophet and their armies are destroyed

"And the beast was captured, and with him the false prophet who did mighty miracles on behalf of the beast—miracles that deceived all who had accepted the mark of the beast and who worshiped his statue. Both the beast and his false prophet were thrown alive into the lake of fire that burns with sulfur. [21]Their entire army was killed by the sharp sword that came out of the mouth of the one riding the white horse. And all the vultures of the sky gorged themselves on the dead bodies" (Revelation 19:20-21).

12. Satan is bound and locked in the pit for one thousand years

"Then I saw an angel come down from heaven with the key to the bottomless pit and a heavy chain in his hand. [2]He seized the dragon—that old serpent, the Devil, Satan—and bound him in chains for a thousand years. ³The angel threw him into the bottomless pit, which he then shut and locked so Satan could not deceive the nations anymore until the thousand years were finished. Afterward he would be released again for a little while" (Revelation 20:1-3).

The Millennial Kingdom

Following this seven-year period of time, with rejoicing in heaven and tribulation on earth, the victorious return of Christ will issue in the millennial kingdom. Christ will rule the world for one thousand years from David's throne.

Revelation 20 uses the phrase "thousand years" six times in referring to the period when Christ will rule his kingdom on earth. Believers raptured from the Church Age, and those who become believers during the Tribulation and are martyred, will reign with Christ.

"Blessed and holy are those who share in the first resurrection. For them the second death holds no power, but they will be priests of God and Christ and reign with him a thousand years" (Revelation 20:6).

Satan will be released after a thousand years and will lead a rebellion on earth.

"When the thousand years end, Satan will be let out of his prison. ⁸He will go out to deceive the nations from every corner of the earth, which are called Gog and Magog. He will gather them together for battle—a mighty host, as numberless as sand along the shore. ⁹And I saw them as they went up on the broad plain of the earth and surrounded God's people and the beloved city. But fire from heaven came down on the attacking armies and consumed them" (Revelation 20:7-9).

Satan will be thrown into the lake of fire forever.

"Then the Devil, who betrayed them, was thrown into the lake of fire that burns with sulfur, joining the beast and the false prophet. There they will be tormented day and night forever and ever" (Revelation 20:10).

The Great White Throne Judgment for all Unbelievers

"And I saw a great white throne, and I saw the one who was sitting on it. The earth and sky fled from his presence, but they found no place to hide. [12]I saw the dead, both great and small, standing before God's throne. And the books were opened, including the Book of Life. And the dead were judged according to the things written in the books, according to what they had done. [13]The sea gave up the dead in it, and death and the grave gave up the dead in them. They were all judged according to their deeds. [14]And death and the grave were thrown into the lake of fire. This is the second death—the lake of fire. [15]And anyone whose name was not found recorded in the Book of Life was thrown into the lake of fire" (Revelation 20:11-15).

A New Heaven and a New Earth Replace the Old

"Then I saw a new heaven and a new earth, for the old heaven and the old earth had disappeared. And the sea was also gone. [2]And I saw the holy city, the new Jerusalem, coming down from God out of heaven like a beautiful bride prepared for her husband.

[3]"I heard a loud shout from the throne, saying, 'Look, the home of God is now among his people! He will live with them, and they will be his people. God himself will be with them. [4]He will remove all of their sorrows, and there will be no more death or sorrow or crying or pain. For the old world and its evils are gone forever.'

[5]"And the one sitting on the throne said, 'Look, I am making all things new!' And then he said to me, 'Write this down, for what I tell you is trustworthy and true.' [6]And he also said, 'It is finished! I am the Alpha and the Omega—the Beginning and the End. To all who are thirsty I will give the springs of the water of life without charge! [7]All who are

victorious will inherit all these blessings, and I will be their God, and they will be my children'" (Revelation 21:1-7).

John then described our eternal home, the New Jerusalem.

"So he [an angel] took me [John] in spirit to a great, high mountain, and he showed me the holy city, Jerusalem, descending out of heaven from God. ¹¹It was filled with the glory of God and sparkled like a precious gem, crystal clear like jasper. ¹²Its walls were broad and high, with twelve gates guarded by twelve angels. And the names of the twelve tribes of Israel were written on the gates. ¹³There were three gates on each side—east, north, south, and west. ¹⁴The wall of the city had twelve foundation stones, and on them were written the names of the twelve apostles of the Lamb.

¹⁵"The angel who talked to me held in his hand a gold measuring stick to measure the city, its gates, and its wall. ¹⁶When he measured it, he found it was a square, as wide as it was long. In fact, it was in the form of a cube, for its length and width and height were each 1,400 miles. ¹⁷Then he measured the walls and found them to be 216 feet thick (the angel used a standard human measure).

¹⁸"The wall was made of jasper, and the city was pure gold, as clear as glass. ¹⁹The wall of the city was built on foundation stones inlaid with twelve gems: the first was jasper, the second sapphire, the third agate, the fourth emerald, ²⁰the fifth onyx, the sixth carnelian, the seventh chrysolite, the eighth beryl, the ninth topaz, the tenth chrysoprase, the eleventh jacinth, the twelfth amethyst.

²¹"The twelve gates were made of pearls—each gate from a single pearl! And the main street was pure gold, as clear as glass.

²²"No temple could be seen in the city, for the Lord God Almighty and the Lamb are its temple. ²³And the city has no need of sun or moon, for the glory of God illuminates the

city, and the Lamb is its light. ²⁴The nations of the earth will walk in its light, and the rulers of the world will come and bring their glory to it. ²⁵Its gates never close at the end of day because there is no night. ²⁶And all the nations will bring their glory and honor into the city. ²⁷Nothing evil will be allowed to enter—no one who practices shameful idolatry and dishonesty—but only those whose names are written in the Lamb's Book of Life.

¹"And the angel showed me a pure river with the water of life, clear as crystal, flowing from the throne of God and of the Lamb, ²coursing down the center of the main street. On each side of the river grew a tree of life, bearing twelve crops of fruit, with a fresh crop each month. The leaves were used for medicine to heal the nations.

³"No longer will anything be cursed. For the throne of God and of the Lamb will be there, and his servants will worship him. ⁴And they will see his face, and his name will be written on their foreheads. ⁵And there will be no night there—no need for lamps or sun—for the Lord God will shine on them. And they will reign forever and ever.

⁶"Then the angel said to me, 'These words are trustworthy and true: the Lord God, who tells his prophets what the future holds, has sent his angel to tell you what will happen soon'" (Revelation 21:10-22:6).

Perhaps we can view the New Jerusalem as a four-sided, crystal pyramid, fourteen hundred miles on each side at its base, rising fourteen hundred miles in the air, to a point where Christ's throne is. The river of the water of life descends from the throne, nourishing along its banks the trees of life, which continually yield twelve different kinds of fruit.

Practical Life Application

The Book of Revelation and the Bible end with a warning not to add or remove anything from the prophecy of God (Revelation 22:18-19). His complete revelation to us is to be taken seriously.

In light of our understanding of biblical prophecy, the imminent return of Christ, with whom we are to reign and live victoriously forever, we should live anticipating His return and be found holy and faithful.

There are four quotes from the Lord Jesus Christ given to us by the apostle John in the final chapter. They are worthy of meditation.

"Look, I am coming soon! Blessed are those who obey the prophecy written in this scroll" (Revelation 22:7).

"See, I am coming soon, and my reward is with me, to repay all according to their deeds. [13]I am the Alpha and the Omega, the First and the Last, the Beginning and the End" (Revelation 22:12-13).

"I, Jesus, have sent my angel to give you this message for the churches. I am both the source of David and the heir to his throne. I am the bright morning star" (Revelation 22:16).

"He who is the faithful witness to all these things says, 'Yes, I am coming soon!' Amen! Come, Lord Jesus! [21]The grace of the Lord Jesus be with you all" (Revelation 22:20-21).

He is coming soon. Perhaps today. Are you ready? Perhaps He has been waiting for you. Have you believed in Christ, putting your faith in Him?

If you have trusted Christ, perhaps this is the time for you to get serious about being His disciple. Spend time with Him. Spend time in His Word. Spend time with His people. If you have just completed this book, you now have knowledge and a resource by which to grow and mature rapidly in your Christian faith. Make Jesus Christ the main priority of your life.

One glorious day we will see Him face to face. May His words to you be the same as the Master in Matthew 25:21; "Well done, my good and faithful servant."

"Amen! Come, Lord Jesus!"

Chaper 15

"Quick Start" for New Believers

"For I know the plans I have for you," says the Lord. "They are plans for good and not for disaster, to give you a future and a hope" (Jeremiah 29:11).

If you recently put your faith in the Lord Jesus Christ as your personal Savior, you might be asking, "Now what?"

A friend or family member may be helping you learn the basics of biblical Christianity. That's great. But if you are not sure what to do next, here are some "quick start" suggestions to help you move along in the right direction on your journey.

First, Let's Review

What did you do? There are many ways of expressing it. You may have "accepted Christ." "Received or invited Him into your heart." "Been saved." Become "born again." Simply, you responded to the "gospel" or good news of Jesus Christ by believing, putting your faith in, trusting Christ, the Son of God, to save you from hell and take you to heaven one day.

What is this "gospel?" In the fifteenth chapter of 1 Corinthians (in the New Testament) the apostle Paul defined it concisely. The gospel by which we are saved is this: Jesus Christ died for our sins and rose from the dead. This is "good news" because:

1. "For all have sinned; all fall short of God's glorious standard" (Romans 3:23).

2. "For the wages of sin is death" (Romans 6:23).

   We are all sinners. We deserve death. We can do nothing to change these facts. So Jesus came and died in our place.

3. "But God showed his great love for us by sending Christ to die for us while we were still sinners" (Romans 5:8).

   Jesus took the penalty we deserve. He took our place. He was our substitute. The only thing left for us is to accept Christ's work on our behalf…to believe in him.

4. "God saved you by his special favor when you believed. And you can't take credit for this; it is a gift from God. Salvation is not a reward for the good things we have done, so none of us can boast about it" (Ephesians 2:8-9).

   God saved you when you trusted Christ. God did it all on His own. We didn't deserve it. Salvation is a gift, received by God's grace, through faith.

Understanding Faith, Belief, and Trust

"For God so loved the world that he gave his one and only Son, that whoever believes in him shall not perish but have eternal life" (John 3:16).

This is more than intellectual acceptance of a fact. You may believe Queen Elizabeth is English, but that does not make you a British citizen. A better way of expressing "belief" or "faith" might be "trust."

Picture yourself driving through a green light without stopping. We believe we are safe as we put our faith in a little piece of colored glass. We're actually trusting a piece of red glass we can't even see to stop someone else from crashing into us. Now that's faith! How much more worthy of our faith and trust is the Son of God, the Lord Jesus Christ.

What Happened?

A lot happened the moment you trusted Christ, facts that will impact your life forever.

1. God was satisfied forever with Christ's sacrifice of His own life for your sins. He substituted Himself for you.

2. You were instantly declared "not guilty" in the court of heaven, justified in God's eyes in a legal sense.

3. You were purchased, that is, redeemed by Christ from slavery to sin and your old way of doing things (Romans 3:21-25).

4. You were "born again" spiritually and given a new life as God the Holy Spirit came to live inside you (John 3:5-7; 1 Corinthians 6:19; Titus 3:5-7; 1 Peter 1:3).

Can I Be Sure This New Life...
Salvation...Is Really Forever?

Jesus said, "I tell you the truth, whoever hears my word and believes him who sent me has eternal life and will not be condemned; he has crossed over from death to life" (John 5:24).

The apostle Paul wrote, "For I am convinced that neither death nor life, neither angels nor demons, neither the present nor the future, nor any powers, neither height nor depth, nor anything else in all creation, will be able to separate us from the love of God that is in Christ Jesus our Lord" (Romans 8:38-39).

The apostle John wrote, "I write these things to you who believe in the name of the Son of God so that you may know that you have eternal life" (1 John 5:13).

This Is Just the Beginning!

Becoming a Christian is the start of a great and wonderful adventure as you learn more about God and come to know Him in a deeply personal way.

"'For I know the plans I have for you,' declares the LORD, 'plans to prosper you and not to harm you, plans to give you hope and a future'" (Jeremiah 29:11).

Let's use our traffic light analogy again. Let's say you've been stopped at a red light for what seems like an eternity. When you put your faith and trust in the Lord Jesus Christ the light turns green so you can go forward.

You may have been told the Bible is your roadmap, but you hardly know how to read it. You have a lot of questions. Do you go straight ahead or turn? How fast should you go? Do you have enough fuel for the trip? What do you do now?

Here's a List of Suggestions
to Get You Going and Growing

1. Start reading the Bible. Get a good Bible translation, one that is easy to understand. Try the New Living Translation (what we use in this material), New International Version, New American Standard Bible, or the New King James Version. There are good reference Bibles such as the Open Bible and the Ryrie Study Bible, with maps and helpful notes. Start by reading the Gospel of John in the New Testament. Then read a few of Paul's letters: Philippians, Ephesians, Galatians, and Romans. Then read the Gospel of Mark. It is a good thing to

schedule some time every day to read. Some people do it early in the morning, while others read before bedtime. Reading the Bible is like listening to God.

Here's what the Bible (Scripture) says about itself. "All Scripture is inspired by God and is useful to teach us what is true and to make us realize what is wrong in our lives. It straightens us out and teaches us to do what is right. It is God's way of preparing us in every way, fully equipped for every good thing God wants us to do" (2 Timothy 3:16-17). The New International Version translates this as "All Scripture is God-breathed."

2. Spend time talking with God. That's what prayer is. You now have a personal relationship with God. He talks with you through his Word, the Bible, and you can talk to Him through prayer. "Don't worry about anything; instead, pray about everything. Tell God what you need, and thank him for all he has done. If you do this, you will experience God's peace, which is far more wonderful than the human mind can understand. His peace will guard your hearts and minds as you live in Christ Jesus" (Philippians 4:6-7).

3. Go to a good Bible-teaching church. God wants all Christians to be part of a good church where you will grow in your understanding of God and the Bible. The normal Sunday service is a celebration of worship in which Christians join together to learn about God and to praise Him. A good church offers more. We all need community. We need Christian friends to encourage and support us, as we do the same for them. This is often found in small groups within a local church.

4. Get involved in discipleship. Joining a local church is an important step in the process of maturing as a Christian. This process is called discipleship. Support your church financially, as you are able to, generously, even cheerfully, out of a grateful heart for what God has already provided for you. Baptism is another part of the process.

This is a public demonstration of your faith in Christ. As you put yourself under the authority of a good church, others will help you discover how God has uniquely prepared and gifted you to serve Him and provide you with opportunities to serve. You may not be ready to teach the Bible yet, but you can set up chairs, bring food to the sick, pray for the hurting, or tell others what God is doing for you. To be a disciple of the Lord Jesus Christ involves a lifestyle of intentional choices to follow Him.

Jesus is the Good Shepherd and we are part of his flock. Let's look at some of the characteristics of a disciple using the acronym **"FLOCKS."**

F—Faith. This is where it starts. Each member of the flock must have put his or her faith and trust in Christ.

L—Love. We are to love Him and one another. Learn to be a forgiving person.

O—Obedience. Jesus said, "If you love me, obey my commandments" (John 14:15). Learn God's biblical truths and apply them in your life.

C—Commitment. Grow in your dedication to the Lord and demonstrate it in your life. Be a good steward of your time and resources.

K—Keeping. Disciples stay connected to Christ by abiding or remaining in fellowship with Him. Be faithful in your time of prayer and Bible study.

S—Serving. Be a grace-based giver and server. Serve others as God has gifted you to do with your abilities, talents, time, and resources.

Flocks Witness. One way or another, your life will be a witness for God. He put His Spirit in you. Make it your goal to let Christ shine His life through you. Determine to live morally and with integrity according to God's principles. Be a good reflection of your heavenly Father. Become a disciple who makes disciples.

Here's a New Way of Thinking and Living for Your New Life

I believe...Jesus Christ, the Son of God, died for me, as my full substitute, paid for all my sins, was buried, raised on the third day, lives in heaven today, and has a plan for my life.

I am...forgiven, redeemed, right with God, born again, a new creature in Christ, with God the Holy Spirit living in me.

I do...desire to yield my will to God's will and allow Jesus Christ to live His life through me, to worship Him, to love God and others, to be a growing disciple, servant, and minister, to proclaim the good news, to make God look good by the way I live, all out of a sincere motivation of humble gratitude for all He has done for me.

May you walk with God all the days of your life and may He bless you greatly.

"Quick Start" for New Believers
by Neil Curran
is available in a pamphlet format at a low cost.
This chapter 15 of the book *Exploring the Basics of Biblical Christianity,* may be duplicated in its entirety by churches, nonprofit organizations, and individuals for the sole purpose of giving away without charge any copies to help disciple new believers in Christ.

The publisher, Biblical Communications, would appreciate written notice of these duplication efforts by the parties involved. Thank you.

Biblical Communications

P.O. Box 293911   Lewisville, Texas 75029   U.S.A.
For more information visit our Web site at
www.biblicalcommunications.com